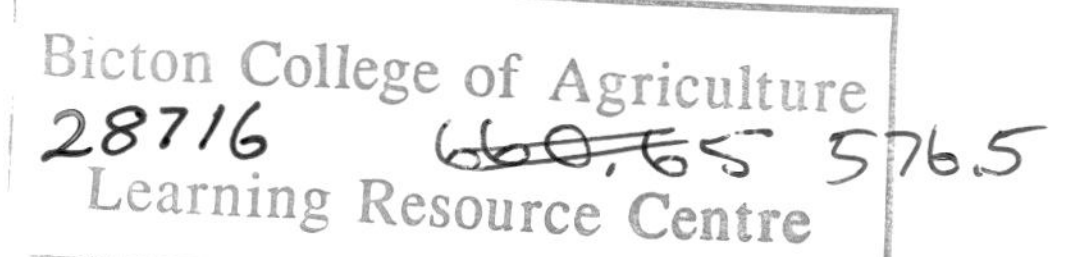

Human and Animal Cloning

ISSUES

Volume 90

Editor

Craig Donnellan

Independence
Educational Publishers
Cambridge

First published by Independence
PO Box 295
Cambridge CB1 3XP
England

British Library Cataloguing in Publication Data
Human and Animal Cloning – (Issues Series)
I. Donnellan, Craig II. Series
660.6'5

ISBN 1 86168 291 3

Printed in Great Britain
MWL Print Group Ltd

Typeset by
Claire Boyd

Cover
The illustration on the front cover is by Pumpkin House.

CONTENTS

Chapter One: Human Cloning

Chapter Two: Animal Cloning

Introduction

Human and Animal Cloning is the ninetieth volume in the Issues series. The aim of this series is to offer up-to-date information about important issues in our world.

Human and Animal Cloning looks at the scientific, ethical and moral issues of cloning.

The information comes from a wide variety of sources and includes:
Government reports and statistics
Newspaper reports and features
Magazine articles and surveys
Website material
Literature from lobby groups
and charitable organisations.

It is hoped that, as you read about the many aspects of the issues explored in this book, you will critically evaluate the information presented. It is important that you decide whether you are being presented with facts or opinions. Does the writer give a biased or an unbiased report? If an opinion is being expressed, do you agree with the writer?

Human and Animal Cloning offers a useful starting-point for those who need convenient access to information about the many issues involved. However, it is only a starting-point. At the back of the book is a list of organisations which you may want to contact for further information.

*****

Human reproductive cloning

The pros and cons

The idea of human reproductive cloning produces a strong response from many people. Producing new genetically identical human beings is a very different proposition to therapeutic cloning.

Arguments for . . .

Some people argue that cloning is the logical next step in reproductive technology. Identical twins are natural clones, so reproductive cloning can be regarded as a technological version of a natural process. If a couple are infertile, why shouldn't they be able to produce clones of themselves? If a couple have lost a child, why shouldn't they be able to replace that loved individual with a clone if that is possible? Equally if someone has made a great contribution to science, music, the arts or literature, it seems like a good idea to produce more of them in the hope that we might benefit even more from what would effectively be a much longer working life. What is more, cloning a child could produce a tissue match for treatment of a life-threatening disease.

. . . and against

Others feel equally strongly that human cloning is completely wrong. With the state of the science as it is at the moment it would involve hundreds of damaged pregnancies to achieve one single live cloned baby. What is more, all the evidence suggests that clones are unhealthy and often have a number of built-in genetic defects which lead to premature ageing and death. It would be completely wrong to bring a child into the world knowing that it was extremely likely to be affected by problems like these. The dignity of human life and the genetic uniqueness we all have would be attacked if cloning became commonplace. People might be cloned unwillingly – we all leave thousands if not millions of cells around every day as we go about our normal lives shedding skin! Who will control who gets cloned? Companies are already making money storing tissue from dead children and partners until the time that human cloning becomes available. How much scope will there be for unscrupulous dealings if human cloning becomes a reality?

Whatever your view, all the evidence is that a clone would not be identical to the original because it would have a different womb environment and would be brought up differently. For example, it would be very galling to clone Einstein and find that the new version didn't like maths!

■ The above information is from the Association of the British Pharmaceutical Industry's Schools website which can be found at www.abpischools.org.uk

Questions on cloning

Information from the World Health Organization

Recent announcements from a number of groups in Asia, Europe, and North America that women under their care have given birth, or are about to give birth, to a 'human clone' have not only produced doubts about the claims but have also reactivated the public debate in this area and raised questions about the facts and ethics of what might be involved in human cloning.

What is a clone?
The term clone, from the Greek for 'twig', denotes a group of identical entities; in recent years, 'clone' has come to mean a member of such a group and, in particular, an organism that is a genetic copy of an existing organism. The term is applied by scientists not only to entire organisms but to molecules (such as DNA) and cells.

Can cloning occur naturally?
Yes, cloning occurs in nature and can occur in organisms that reproduce sexually as well as those that reproduce asexually. Many species produce their descendants asexually, that is, without the combining of the male and female genetic material that occurs in sexual reproduction, and these offspring are clones of their parent. Mammals, however, do not normally reproduce asexually, and the birth of the lamb Dolly at a research institute in Scotland in 1996 was the first reported mammalian clone produced asexually. In sexual reproduction, clones are, however, created when a fertilised egg splits to produce identical (monozygous) twins with identical DNA.

Would cloning produce identical people?
It is not possible to answer this question with certainty because the experiments required to answer this question have not been carried out, but experience with mammalian cloning suggests that the answer is 'no'. If successful, somatic-cell nuclear transfer (SCNT) could allow the production of one (or many more) individuals who are, genetically, virtually identical to one another and to the individual whose cell nucleus was used to produce them. This does not mean they would be identical physically or in personality, just as monozygous twins are not identical either, because the development of an organism is influenced by the interaction of its genes and its environment. In the case of human clones, this environment would differ from the moment that each was created, implanted in a uterus, gestated, and born. Furthermore, in all of the species of mammals cloned thus far – including mice, rabbits, pigs and cattle as well as sheep – unpredictable genetic and epigenetic problems have arisen which have not only led to a high rate of abnormalities and prenatal death but have also created health problems for most of the animals born alive, problems which differ from one clone to another.

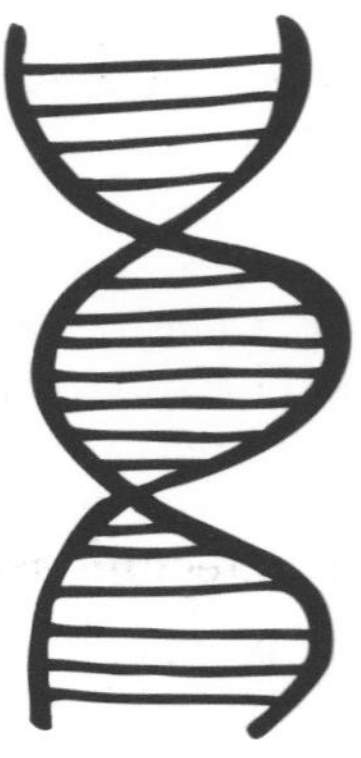

Why did scientists develop cloning techniques?
Scientists were initially interested in SCNT as a means of determining whether all the genes in an organism's genome remain functional even after most of them have been switched off as a developing organism's cells assume their specialised functions as blood, bone, muscle, and so forth. The ability of scientists to stimulate the DNA in a nucleus from a fully differentiated cell that has been transferred to an enucleated egg to revert to a condition comparable to the DNA in a newly fertilised egg and to begin the process of embryonic development demonstrated that all the genes remain viable in differentiated cells even though only a few genes are actually expressed in each cell. Commercial interest in animal cloning centres on the replication of large numbers of genetically identical animals, especially those derived from a progenitor which has been modified genetically. In this fashion, mice or other laboratory animals that exhibit particular conditions can be created for specialised studies, or herds of farm animals (such as goats, sheep, or cows) can be created all of whom produce pharmaceutically useful proteins in their milk.

Does the term 'human cloning' have a single meaning?
No. Current controversy about the creation of a 'human clone' concerns the possibility of replicating a human being (living or deceased) through the SCNT technique used to create Dolly, but the term is used in several other ways.

First, 'human clone' can also be applied to the creation of genetically identical siblings, such as those which occur naturally in identical twins and which has also been attempted experimentally by scientists through the splitting of embryos at the two to eight cell stage of development (sometimes called a blastomere or 'pre-embryo'). Embryo-splitting has been used for some time in artificial breeding programmes for farm animals like cattle. In a 1993 experiment, scientists in Washington, DC, turned 17 non-viable human embryos into 48. These embryos were cultured for some days and then discarded. If embryos created through such splitting were implanted and brought to term simultaneously, they would be comparable to monozygous twins. If a human blastomere were split and one of the resulting embryos were brought to term while the others were frozen (a common contemporary technique in fertility clinics) and implanted and born at a later date, the result would be 'serial twins'. Although genetically identical, such individuals would differ from ordinary twins because they would be born at different times (and perhaps even to different mothers); moreover, the decision to implant the later-born serial twin(s) might be based on evaluating the 'fitness' or other characteristics of the first-born, and predictions about the life course of the later-born twin(s) might be based on experience with the pre-existing one.

The term 'human cloning' can also be applied to the creation of embryos through SCNT not to produce offspring but for use as a scientific tool. In particular, these non-reproductive uses of cloning – sometimes termed 'research cloning' or 'therapeutic cloning' to differentiate them from cloning for reproductive purposes – are being pursued as a means of creating human embryonic stem cells for scientific study and eventually for therapeutic purposes. Once cloned embryos have reached the blastocyst stage (approximatively 5 days after fertilisation), the inner cell mass, from which stem cell lines are derived, is removed; in the process, the embryo is destroyed. Some scientists engaged in this work prefer to describe it using the term 'somatic-cell nuclear transfer to create stem cells', because they feel that the term 'cloning' connotes the creation of a child. Critics of this position say that 'cloning' is the appropriate term because the suggestion of two procedures is spurious; it is better to say that the same technique – the creation of embryos through SCNT – can have two different outcomes, the production of embryonic stem cells and the production of babies.

What justifications are offered for non-reproductive human cloning?

Scientists engaged in cloning for research argue that it presents a unique method for studying genetic changes in cells derived from patients suffering from such diseases as Parkinson's disease, Alzheimer's disease, and diabetes. Scientists interested in therapeutic cloning look ahead to the day when they believe that embryonic stem cells will be used to assist drug development and evaluation, for diagnostic purposes, and to create cells and tissues for transplantation. For the latter, if the stem cells used in transplantation were derived from embryos cloned from the patient needing the transplant, they might be less subject to rejection, since their DNA would be nearly identical to the patient's own. Whether human embryonic stem cells hold unique therapeutic promise – as opposed to stem cells from adult tissues – and, if so, whether the creation of cloned embryos as a source of stem cells would add to their therapeutic value – are matters of ongoing debate in scientific circles.

Scientists engaged in cloning for research argue that it presents a unique method for studying genetic changes in cells derived from patients suffering from such diseases as Parkinson's disease

What uses are suggested for human reproductive cloning?

Proponents of human reproductive cloning argue that it would enlarge the current spectrum of assisted reproductive techniques. In particular, men who do not produce gametes could have children who inherit their genome. In such a case, if the egg came from the wife, the couple would not have to involve a third 'parent' (the sperm donor) in producing their child. Women who do not produce eggs could also have children carrying their genetic information (although they would need a donor egg) and the child would not receive a genetic contribution from the male partner. (In the case of lesbian couples, one might provide the egg, with its mitochondrial DNA, and the other the nuclear DNA.) Other reasons offered for using SCNT to create children include: to produce a child with certain genetic features (who could, for example, serve as a bone marrow donor for a diseased sibling); to replicate a deceased child or other loved one; to fulfil the desire for a child based on an admired 'prototype'; or to achieve 'immortality' by living on through one's clone. All of these scenarios raise ethical, legal and social issues.

What ethical arguments have been raised concerning human reproductive cloning?

Whereas widespread consensus exists among the public and policy makers internationally against reproductive cloning, arguments pro and con have been presented. The main arguments brought forward against human reproductive cloning are:

■ Physical harm:
Experience with animal cloning has shown substantial risks of debilitating and even lethal conditions occurring in the fetuses produced using these techniques that cannot be individually predicted and avoided. Some of these conditions also present a considerable risk for the gestational mother carrying the cloned animals to term. On the basis of this information, human reproductive cloning would – at this point – constitute a risky experiment that is not sufficiently backed up by successful laboratory and animal research. It would clearly not meet the usual ethical standards in biomedical research. Indeed, the risk-benefit ratio is so grave that in any other biomedical field, such as the development of a new pharmaceutical, no ethical researcher would proceed to a human trial based on the current preclinical results in reproductive cloning.

■ Research standards:
Responsible biomedical researchers not only engage in thorough laboratory and animal studies before proceeding with human subjects but also submit each step of their work to scientific appraisal through open dissemination of their results in scientific meetings and peer-reviewed journals. Such transparency, which is

especially important when scientists operate in private institutions – without day-to-day interaction with colleagues and institutional leaders who are able to bring independent judgement to the design and conduct of the research – has been largely lacking in the reproductive cloning experiments announced thus far.

■ Autonomy:
Any child created through SCNT would be unable to give consent to the experiment. Although the same problem arises in any research on the unborn or young children, cloning research is different because, unlike situations in which parents give permission for an experimental intervention that aims to correct an existing problem in a fetus or child, no patient (and hence no problem) exists prior to the cloning experiment. An issue of autonomy would also arise if a person's DNA were used to create one or more copies without that person's permission or perhaps even without his or her knowledge.

■ Dignity:
The Universal Declaration on Human Genome and Human Rights (UNESCO 1997) as well as many other documents state that reproductive cloning is contrary to human dignity. This position is mainly based on the following ethical considerations:

a. cloning is an asexual mode of reproduction, which is unnatural for the human species; a cloned individual will not have two genetic parents; generation lines and family relationships would be distorted.

b. cloning limits the lottery of heredity, which is an essential component in ensuring that each human life (or lives, in the case of monozygous twins) begins as something that has never existed before.

c. cloning furthers an instrumental attitude toward human beings, that is, that people exist to serve purposes set by other people. When cloning is used in this fashion, dignity is undermined in two different but related ways – first, a clone's right to an individual life-course will be constrained by others' expectations that he or she will behave in certain ways (based on experience with the genetic progenitor's life), and second, the clone may not (or may not wish to) behave in those ways, because behaviour is not shaped by genes alone, and will hence disappoint others' expectations and suffer the consequences.

d. especially in conjunction with other means of genetic modification, cloning risks turning human beings into manufactured objects; this is not only contrary to human dignity but unwise, as human beings lack the prescience to meddle successfully with evolution and genetic diversity in this fashion.

■ Justice:
Health care resources should be devoted instead to other health or research needs that address more urgent problems than any associated with reproductive cloning; furthermore, not only are there few if any people for whom reproductive cloning would offer the only means of establishing a family, but if it became established as an assisted reproductive technology, it would probably only be available to a small group of privileged individuals with the financial resources to afford it.

■ Conflicts of interest:
Special ethical problems would arise if researchers had a financial interest in the outcome of the studies they conduct with human subjects; for this reason, such interests are usually disallowed by ethical standards or, where they are unavoidable, special expectations of openness and independent review of research are required.

■ Psychological/social harm:
The cloned individual may suffer psychological harm from its status as being a genetic 'copy' of somebody else. The clone might be dominated by the person who creates him or her, unduly constrained by expectations based on the abilities or life course of the donor, or stigmatised by society. It is not certain that these concerns can be effectively addressed by education and legislation.

The main arguments brought forward for human reproductive cloning are:

■ Beneficence: A new treatment option could be offered to infertile couples. Predetermining the genetic make-up would allow selection of desirable traits.

■ Autonomy: People should be free in their reproductive decisions; the state or international organisations do not have the right to interfere with reproductive autonomy.

Adult cell or reproductive cloning

The nucleus from a normal body cell of an adult animal is placed into an empty ovum and allowed to develop into an 'identical twin' of the original animal. The first and most famous adult cell clone of a large mammal was Dolly the sheep. The great medical hopes for this technology are to be able to reproduce many genetically engineered organisms to make therapeutic proteins, and possibly to help overcome human infertility problems.

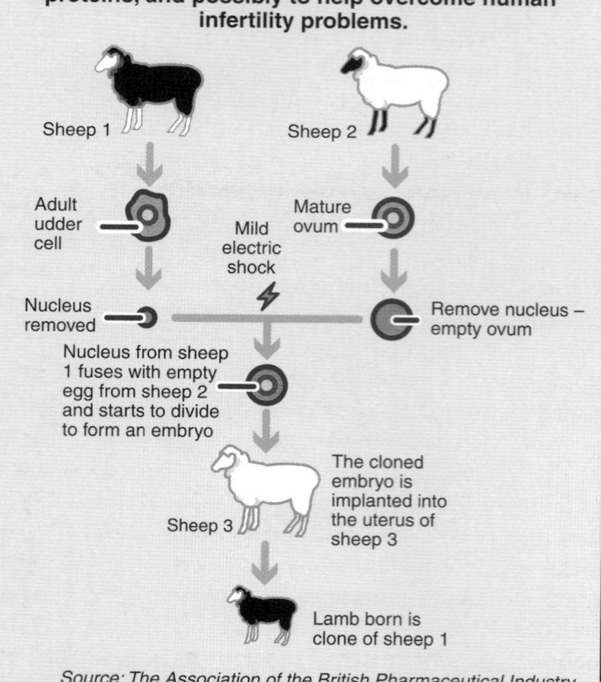

Source: The Association of the British Pharmaceutical Industry

Human cloning

Information from the ProLife Party

The beginning of a new member of the human species occurs when a one-cell embryo is produced from the fusion of sperm and ovum. Human cloning produces an embryo by fusing the nucleus of an adult cell with an enucleated ovum. A new zygote (single-cell human being) is formed by this process, and that young human being will be a near genetic copy of the adult cell donor.

As soon as a human individual exists, he or she has rights and interests relating to his or her own future – however long or short that future may be. Embryos have an interest in survival and protection from attack, just like any human being.

Human beings are valuable in themselves, simply as human beings. We have dignity in virtue of what we are, not what we do. To see human beings as having dignity only on the basis of current functional abilities – abilities we arbitrarily select – is to fail to recognise that human rights are intrinsic to the individual. The notion of human rights makes no sense without the notion that each of us has dignity in virtue of what we are.

To deliberately produce a human being with the express intention of destroying that same human being is, therefore, totally unethical. Moreover, to make a human being the product of technological manufacture is to treat that human being in a way that already demeans him/her. The manufacture of human beings encourages people to treat those human beings as less than human, as can be seen in the fact that thousands are killed or otherwise abused every day in IVF clinics around the world.

With so-called 'therapeutic' cloning, embryos are killed by extracting their cells when they are 5-7 days old. With so-called 'reproductive' cloning, embryos are, in theory at least, transferred to a woman's body, gestated and brought to birth. The British Government

proudly proclaims that it has outlawed 'reproductive' cloning – i.e., the transfer of clone embryos. However, it is not the transfer but the creation of clones which should be outlawed as degrading to human beings. Interestingly, Dolly's creator, Ian Wilmut, now supports not only lethal but live-birth human cloning, despite his doubts about the latter just a few years ago. Perhaps he should ponder his own words at the time: 'It does not follow, just because we grow used to some phenomenon or other, that that phenomenon is good. We grow used to bad things, as well as to good.'

As soon as a human individual exists, he or she has rights and interests relating to his or her own future

The justification put forward for lethal experimental cloning is that by destroying clone embryos we will obtain embryonic stem cells for use in treating those with conditions such as Parkinson's. This claim is not even sustained by the scientific community at large. The *New Scientist*, for example, wisely noted: 'Will tailor-made, cloned stem cells be needed for treating Parkinson's? Almost certainly not: of all the body's organs, the brain is the least likely to reject imperfectly matched tissues.' But most importantly, even if this research were likely to succeed, how can we justify the wilful destruction of one human life in an attempt to save another?

We welcome the development of ethically acceptable treatments for conditions such as Parkinson's and are greatly encouraged by the use of adult stem cells, which can be extracted without killing anyone, have already produced successful treatments for a range of conditions, and have none of the potential tumour-forming problems that are inherent to embryonic stem cells.

■ The above information is from the ProLife Party. For further information visit their website which can be found at www.prolife.org.uk

Cloning

Anthony McCarthy

Cloning means the production of a living being that is genetically identical to the one from which it originated. Specifically, human cloning is the artificial production of a genetic replica of another human being. This is achieved without the contribution of two gametes (sperm and ovum), and is therefore a form of asexual reproduction. Whereas IVF is a form of reproduction achieved by fertilisation of an ovum (egg) by a sperm outside the body, sperm is not used in cloning.

One way in which cloning could take place is by somatic cell nuclear transfer. Here, the nucleus of an unfertilised ovum is removed and replaced with the nucleus of a somatic cell, or whole diploid body cell, from a developed embryo, foetus or adult individual. The ovum is then stimulated either chemically or by an electrical pulse to create a human embryo. Given that the nucleus contains almost all of a cell's genetic material, the new embryo will be a delayed genetic twin/clone of the human individual from whom the cell was taken. In this whole process male sexuality plays no direct role.

Purposes of cloning

The above-described cloning technique, if successfully applied to human individuals, will produce a new human being at its embryonic stage of development. This makes it clear that all human cloning is, in fact, reproductive. The term 'reproductive cloning' is therefore a tautology.

Aside from the definition of cloning as a technical procedure, it has become commonplace to define cloning in terms of the purposes for which it is done. These 'definitions by aim' need to be carefully analysed. Nowadays there is much talk of 'reproductive cloning' and 'therapeutic cloning', as though they were different types of cloning. They are not. 'Therapeutic cloning' refers to the production by cloning of a human embryo for the purpose of using that individual as a source of cells or for experimentation that may offer therapeutic benefits to other human beings. The term is manipulative because it obscures the fact that such interventions carried out on the early clone human embryo are never therapeutic for that individual, who, as a result of having cells extracted from it at an early stage, will die.

For the sake of clarity, and given the fact that all cloning is reproductive in itself, I will refer to cloning for research/transplantation (or experimental cloning), and cloning for birth (or live-birth cloning). In the term cloning for birth is included both cloning done with the intention to implant and bring to birth, and also any implantation of a clone embryo for this purpose.

Cloning for birth

An example of cloning for birth has been given with the case of Dolly the sheep. In a human case it would mean implanting a clone embryo in the uterus of a woman whose ovum had been used for cloning, or in the uterus of a surrogate mother, with the intention that the clone child be carried to term. This new individual human being, barring genetic mutation, should produce a body structure similar to that of its adult cell donor. Cloning for birth has, among other things, been proposed as a way for women suffering from infertility to obtain clone children. These children, commissioned by and cloned from the infertile woman, would be produced using another

woman's ovum, then implanted, gestated and born through either the commissioning mother or a surrogate.

Given what we presently know from animal cloning, it is clear that this procedure would cause physical harm to human clones. Many of these human beings would have severe genetic or other disabilities, which might only become apparent at late stages of pregnancy. Many babies would miscarry and those making it to birth would be likely to suffer premature death or major health problems caused by the means used to produce them. Nearly all scientists working in the field would accept this. On top of these problems, clone human beings who were discovered in the womb to be disabled would be at a much higher risk of being destroyed through deliberate abortion.

Women choosing to gestate clone children would be exposed to grave physical and psychological harm. The high rate of miscarriage would carry health risks for the mother, aside from the trauma that would result from either miscarriage or neonatal death. Observation of animal clones has shown that malformed or oversized foetuses could constitute a direct physical threat to the gestational mother. In such cases as these, as well as in cases of genetic disability, mothers would be under pressure to abort the child they were carrying. Abortion, in addition to taking the life of the child, would carry health risks for the mother, both physical and psychological.

Procreation

The most obvious threat posed by somatic cell nuclear transfer cloning is to the nature of human procreation and the rearing of children. Cloning, as a form of asexual reproduction, completely displaces the procreative act between a man and a woman. As human beings we are bodily beings. Our living bodies are intrinsic to our unified personal experience. Sexual procreation between a man and a woman is a single act performed by a pair. In this regard the man and woman form, in the words of philosopher Germain Grisez, a single reproductive (or procreative) principle. It is because as persons we are

Cloning, as a form of asexual reproduction, completely displaces the procreative act between a man and a woman

a dynamic unity of body and soul that our bodily acts carry an inherent meaning. In light of the couple forming a single reproductive principle, we can see that an organic unity of persons is present in the procreative type of act. The meaning of these acts is therefore not absolutely reducible to the personal projects of the couple. These acts have an inherent connection to the good of the transmission of life. To deny this and to claim that the meaning of sexual union is determined simply by the desire/will of the couple, is to deny the basic purpose of sexual union between a man and a woman, and with it the normative meanings of our sexual differentiation and complementarity.

By giving themselves in love to each other and bringing together their gametes (sperm and ovum) through a personal sexual act, the couple each give genes to form a completely new human individual. The new human is genetically unique, related to the parents but distinct from them. He has come to be as a result of the procreative act of his parents and his genetic make-up is unpredictable. He is genetically linked to the past, yet open to the future. These features carry the valuable message that the child is the gift and fruit of sexual procreation, who, as such, must be unconditionally accepted in all his contingent and unplanned characteristics. He is not produced or chosen as a particular child with particular features according to a particular template. He is not custom-made according to the will of his parents. The fact that the child is a unique and contingent gift, the result of sexual union, invites acceptance of a different yet equal and related person, not someone the parents own, or who exists only for their own purposes. The sense that a child is not a possession is an important one for parents to have, lest they be tempted to treat him as if he were. In rearing a child the parents should guide and to some extent mould the child, but only so that he or she may develop a truly separate identity from them.

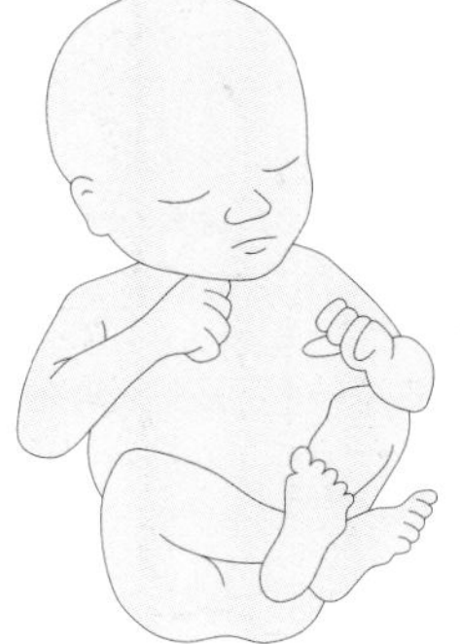

Production

The clone child will not come to be as the result of a sexual act between two persons, but will be produced in a laboratory following a series of separate acts. These acts will include the extracting of an adult cell, the extracting of a woman's ovum and removal of its nucleus, the technical procedure of fusing the cell with the enucleated ovum in vitro, the transferral of the early embryo to a woman's womb. At no point could there be said to be, in any of these acts, an organic unity of persons. Each act is part of a production process. The child is brought into being according to set criteria, in this case with a pre-selected genetic pattern. Thus the 'parents' of the clone have, or aim at having, complete control over what type of child they are to have in the same way a producer has complete control over a product. A child produced by such methods is thus reduced to the status of an object of the producers' will. This inequality of relation, whereby producers wilfully place themselves in a position of dominion over the product, is radically opposed both to the meaning of procreative acts and to the equality and dignity of the child. Such a choice is therefore intrinsically wrong. Putting oneself in the position of producer greatly increases the temptation to value one's child according to how he/she measures up to one's requirements.

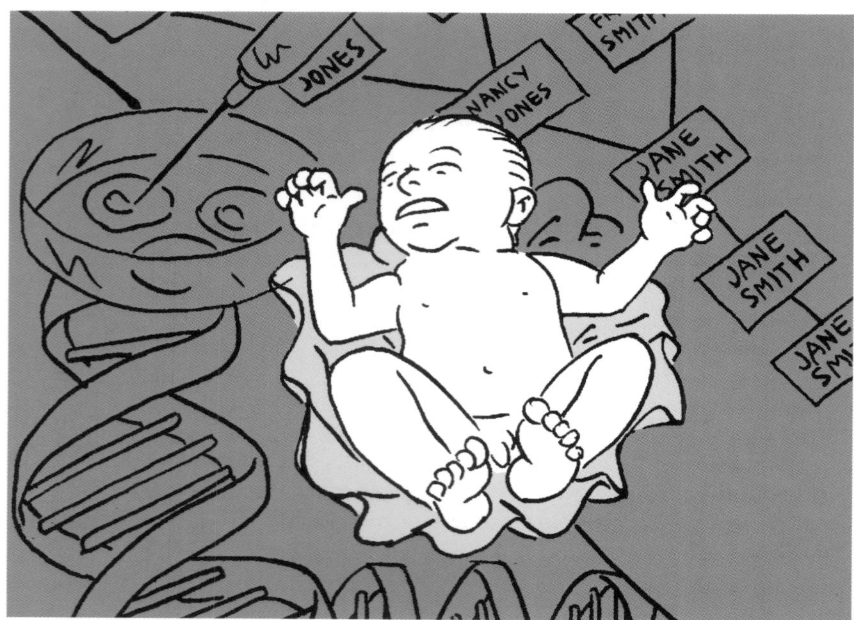

Identity

The clone child, while being a near genetic replica of the adult cell donor, will be an entirely separate individual. We are not reducible, as human persons, to our genes. Human identical twins occurring in nature are closer to each other genetically than a clone and its adult cell donor would be, but remain completely separate persons and undergo separate experiences. Radical similarities between persons do not make them identical as persons. One can only talk of similarity against a background of difference.

But the point is not that a clone would not be a distinct person from his/her adult cell donor. It is rather that he/she will have been deliberately produced as a replica of another human, and thus will appear to be a replacement copy of someone, and not a unique original. To attempt to replicate someone genetically is to attempt something that radically removes genetic differences between people. Such differences certainly symbolise the uniqueness and separateness of persons, and protect us against the idea of treating people as replaceable. Cloning, which makes mass replication possible, would undermine this important symbolism and thereby handicap the formation of a sense of individual identity.

Our genetic uniqueness helps us to have a sense of our essential uniqueness, and carries with it the message that we have the possibility of living a life that is fully our own. The clone is denied this option insofar as he is, genetically, re-enacting another's life. The clone's possibility of self-determination, a value our present society claims to respect, would be undermined given that he could always be compared to the one from whom he was formed. In many cases he will have been formed precisely in order to resemble an original. He will live life in the shadow of his original whose actual development could be used as a template in the clone's rearing.

Even if the clone were never to meet his or her original, the very awareness of such a person's existence would lead to a sense of living in the shadow of this unknown person. To argue, as some advocates of cloning do, that it is best to keep the clone in ignorance of how he came to be, is implicitly to admit the existence of the very problem that those who oppose cloning have pointed out.

Motherhood and identity

The formation of a sense of identity is deeply influenced by familial relations. The clone has no father as such. A single woman could take an adult cell from herself and have it fused with one of her enucleated eggs thereby producing a clone of herself who will be even closer to her genetically than a clone who is not made using her ovum. She will then be the belated genetic twin-sister, as well as the birth mother, of the clone child. How, one may ask in a case such as this, is the child to develop any sort of self-identity? The choices made by the single woman will deliberately deprive the clone child of both a genetic and a social father, thereby distorting that child's relations with the male sex.

In another case a clone could come to be with a partial genetic mother (whose enucleated ovum is fused with an adult donor cell to create the clone embryo), a gestational mother (in whose uterus the clone will be implanted and brought to birth) and a commissioning mother (who ordered the clone). Are these separate people to be regarded as quasi-parents, and what duties do they have to the clone child they helped to bring about? Which one is duty bound, for the sake of the child, to take on the role of social mother? The genetic mother is not a genetic mother in the ordinary sense, in that she will not have contributed a haploid set of chromosomes to the baby, but will only have provided an enucleated ovum, thereby contributing only mitochondrial genes. The gestational mother will, again, be only a partial mother to a child that is not fully her own and in whose creation she played no part. The commissioning 'mother' may become the social mother, but has no prior claim which could trump that of the woman who gives birth.

The distancing of the gestational mother from the partial genetic mother of the child in the case of cloning shows up the radical fragmentation and limitation of maternity, not to mention the obliteration of paternity. What would be the duties of the adult cell donor toward his/her younger genetic twin? These questions arise, at least in part, because the clone has been denied real parents. If the 'genetic mother' providing the ovum is also the gestational mother, we still have a case of partial surrogacy, because the ovum provider's genetic contribution is absolutely minimal. She carries a child who is almost entirely formed by the genetic contribution of another. In the case of a donated egg being fused with an adult donor cell following which the clone is implanted into another woman to gestate, a further gap is introduced, a further confusion as to who the mother is. All of these factors serve to remove from the child those traditional ties to parents which can act as a protection against his or her maltreatment. This situation, coupled with the inherent meaning of the production process that has been used to create the clone, leave the clone vulnerable to many types of abuse.

Familial relations

Clone children, like adopted children or those conceived with donor gametes, will have a perfectly reasonable desire to find out their genetic heritage. In the case of the clone there will be a desire to discover and meet one's genetic older twin, assuming that one is being raised outside this person's family. Human experience gives the lie to the belief that genetic inheritance is absolutely irrelevant, and that social parentage is all that matters. At present there are men and women who 'donate' sperm or ova for the creation of children they ensure will never have any social connection with them. This has already become big business, with desirable males/females being able to charge extra for their gametes to be used. 'Donor' offspring are thus robbed of their rightful inheritance in terms of parental care. Cloning, as well as degrading the clone, will simply exacerbate this iniquitous situation, further entrenching the idea that one generation can prosper at the expense of the next.

Even if the clone were never to meet his or her original, the very awareness of such a person's existence would lead to a sense of living in the shadow of this unknown person

■ This extract is from A. McCarthy: *Cloning* (Linacre/CTS Explanations series, 2003)

■ The above information is from the Linacre Centre for Healthcare Ethics' website: www.linacre.org

Why is it dangerous to clone humans?

By Ian Sample

When Panos Zavos, a US fertility specialist, declared January 2004 that he had implanted a cloned embryo into a 35-year-old woman, scientists boiled over with disgust. If there is any truth to the claim – and there is no evidence to suggest so – Zavos's attempt at human cloning was downright dangerous, they chorused. The child would die in the womb or be born with severe abnormalities, they said.

The warning is supported by the high failure rates reported for cloning animals. According to Wolf Reik, of the Babraham Institute, Cambridge, around 99% of clones die in the womb or suffer genetic abnormalities.

But what goes wrong? The problem is that the DNA used to make the clone is taken from cells that aren't meant to create embryos. Zavos said he took DNA from the skin cell of a man and put it in a hollowed-out egg, which was then implanted.

When a cell matures and turns into a particular cell type, such as skin, it programmes its own DNA to express the right genes at the right time to become, and remain, a skin cell. This is done in two ways. Firstly, chemical compounds are tagged on to the central protein thread (chromatin) that DNA is wrapped around. Second, compounds called methyl groups latch on to specific genes, governing when and if each gene is switched on or off. The way the DNA is programmed is different for every tissue type.

The problem is that the DNA used to make the clone is taken from cells that aren't meant to create embryos

It's no surprise, then, that skin cell DNA can lead to appalling defects if used to grow an embryo. 'You get the wrong pattern of gene activity during development, so the clone dies early in the womb or has developmental abnormalities when it is born,' says Reik.

But the very fact that some cloned animals are born, at least superficially, quite healthy, suggests that every now and again, the DNA is able to 'forget' what kind of cell it used to be and apply itself to making an embryo. Scientists know it is chemicals in the body of the hollowed-out egg that help reprogramme the DNA, but quite how remains a mystery.

Harry Griffin, deputy director of the Roslin Institute, which gave us Dolly the sheep, says claims that genetic abnormalities produced by the cloning process can be detected before birth are nonsense. 'There's no way you could pick up some of these subtle, but life-threatening defects,' he says.

There may be another barrier to human cloning. Some studies have suggested that clones born successfully have a biological age the same as the animal that donated the DNA. 'It could mean you age far more quickly,' says Reik.

Scientists lobby the UN to ban cloning

Scientists from four continents will gather at the United Nations this week (2 June 2004) to campaign for a ban on the cloning of babies.

They hope to persuade ambassadors to break a diplomatic deadlock over achieving a worldwide ban on the technique without curbing research on the cloning of early human embryos, which has the potential to lead to new treatments.

Among those who will speak at the event are Prof Ian Wilmut, of the Roslin Institute, near Edinburgh, the first to clone from an adult cell.

Other speakers will include Dr Woo Suk Hwang, the Korean scientist who first cloned a human embryo, and one of the most prominent patients who could benefit from this research, the actor Christopher Reeve, who will provide a taped introduction.

'There will be absolute unanimity on reproductive cloning,' said Prof Wilmut. 'If you attempted to clone a person now, it would result in late abortions and dead children.'

Equally, he is adamant that using cloning as a route to stem cells, master cells in the body, offers such great medical potential that this therapeutic form of cloning early embryos must not be banned. He is preparing a proposal to do such work himself.

A significant number of countries back the 'Costa Rican proposal', notably the United States, which would have outlawed both human reproductive and therapeutic cloning, ending research on a wide range of treatments.

The US position is 'an enormous handicap for the field', said Prof Wilmut. US biomedical research is already 'severely limited' in embryonic stem cell research.

Because it represents a significant proportion of the world's research, the US administration is slowing the development of a range of new treatments for heart disease, diabetes and other illnesses.

If the US lifted the ban on funding for embryo and cloning research, there would be a huge surge in the research, said Prof Wilmut. Even if the UN adopted the Costa Rican proposal, it would not be mandatory in the UK.

However, Prof Wilmut said the decision would offer powerful support for the pro-life movement, which opposes all forms of cloning, and influence discussions in Europe that may also hinder research.

Prof Wilmut and the other scientists back the Belgian convention, which aims to ban human reproductive cloning but would allow individual states to decide whether to legislate against therapeutic cloning.

Supporters argue that, despite the potential benefits of therapeutic cloning, the different views about the ethics of research on early human embryos in different countries makes unanimity on this issue difficult.

Policy on therapeutic cloning should therefore be determined at national level. The effort to lobby UN delegates is led by Bernard Siegel, a Florida-based lawyer.

'A UN vote to ban this important scientific research would be tragic and destroy the hopes of millions suffering from Alzheimer's, Parkinson's, diabetes, cancer, spinal cord injuries, heart disease and other devastating conditions,' he said.

A spokesman for the Michael J Fox Foundation for Parkinson's Research said: 'As a leading funder of cell replacement research in Parkinson's disease, the foundation supports this effort to provide credible information to UN policy makers and the public that draws a distinct line between scientific research that seeks to alleviate human suffering and potential reproductive cloning, which we oppose.'

After two narrow votes on the issue, the last in December 2003, the UN decided to delay discussion until later this year. The Royal Society, the national academy of science, has already started lobbying the British Government.

Lord May, the president, said: 'Research into therapeutic cloning has the potential to help millions of people worldwide because it could help us to develop stem cell treatments and cures.

'We hope that the UN General Assembly recognises that individual countries should be allowed to decide for themselves about the ethical issues surrounding therapeutic cloning.

'However, if the United Nations votes for an extreme ban that outlaws this promising area of research, we urge the UK Government not to sign the convention.'

Cloning is beneficial

By Tae Hoon H.

Imagine a world full of 'Mini-Hitlers', genetic replicates of Adolf Hitler, seeking world domination. Picture them starting a second Holocaust on a worldwide scale, killing millions upon millions of people as a 'final solution' to establish a superior race. This scenario is far-fetched, but this is the kind of thing people think about when they hear the word 'cloning'.

Cloning has always been considered science fiction. Millions of people have enjoyed stories about a sinister use of cloning technology to conquer the world, probably because they hadn't expected cloning to become reality. The creation of Dolly, a cloned sheep, shocked people, including US federal government. The House of Representatives and the Senate immediately drafted bills to completely ban human cloning. President Clinton instituted a moratorium on federal funds for human cloning experiments. He also established the National Bioethics Advisory Commission (NBAC) to address the science and ethics of human cloning. It immediately published an article entitled 'Cloning Human Beings: Report and Recommendations of the NBAC', which basically said human cloning is morally unacceptable.

Several states have also established restrictions on human cloning; one state has even banned human cloning. These government actions are irrational and should be immediately revoked. The federal government should regulate, not ban, human cloning. This is because significant benefits can result from cloning technology. The ethical implications are also only temporary. They are induced by misconception. Besides, fanatic biologists are going to pursue human cloning technology with or without government consent.

It would be beneficial if I begin by briefly explaining the history of cloning and the processes involved. Dolly was given birth in February 1997. She was created by Ian Wilmut and his colleagues at Roslin Institute in Scotland. She was created using a technique called 'somatic-cell nuclear transfer'. This is where a nucleus-omitted ovum is injected by a nucleus taken from a body cell. A jolt of electricity allows the reconstructed egg to divide. The egg is then inserted into a uterus to develop. This is the way the first human clone will mostly likely be made.

Education will change people's negative attitude towards human cloning. If we give human cloning a chance, it will most likely become a part of our daily lives

Numerous of remarkable benefits can come from cloning technology. One of these is a treatment for infertility. Infertility is caused by genetic defects, injuries to the reproductive organs, congenital defects and exposure to toxic substances and radiation. Many assisted-reproduction technologies have been developed. This includes surrogate mothers for women without a functional uterus, intracytoplasmic sperm injection for males who can't produce viable sperm, and IVF for women with blocked or missing fallopian tubes. However, these treatments have proven to be highly inefficient and they can't help people whose reproductive organs have not developed or have been removed. Twelve million Americans are infertile at child-bearing age. They will pursue years of painful and expensive treatments to have little chance of success. Human cloning can offer infertile people a higher chance of success. Most people are infertile because they can't produce viable gametes. Cloning technology wouldn't require viable sperm or egg, any body cell would do. This technology would be able to bypass defective gametes and allow infertile people to have their own biological children. Cloning technology may even prevent clinical depression, divorce, and suicide among infertile people. This is because infertility often leads to them.

Cloning technology can help 'perfect' gene therapy, the actual correction or replacement of defective gene sequences. Gene therapy is currently limited because of inefficient vectors, or viruses that convey new genes into cells. A copy of a defective gene is in every cell of the body. These viruses must infect every one of these cells and replace the defective genes with the normal genes. However, these vectors only infect a frustrating small amount of cells. This deems gene therapy inefficient. Human cloning can change this. Scientists can determine which cells received the desired gene alteration using fluorescent tags; the cells that were affected would glow. Cloning technology would allow scientists to take a cell that had its genome modified and use it to produce an offspring. The resulting child and its descendants would carry the corrected gene in every cell. Cloning technology may be able cure Tay-Sachs disease, cystic fibrosis, muscular dystrophy, and Huntington's disease.

Another benefit of human cloning is that it will allow scientists to better understand cell differentiation. Research on the basic processes of cell differentiation can lead to dramatic new medical interventions. Cell differentiation is where a stem cell, found inside embryos during the first two weeks of development, specialises into cells that perform specific functions. These cells have the potential to develop into any type of cell in the human body. Biologists do not know which internal/external factors induces a stem cell to develop into a specialised cell, whether it be a muscle cell or a nerve cell. A better understanding of cell differentiation will allow biologists to transform stem cells into whichever cell that he/she desires. Burn and spinal cord injury victims might be provided with artificially produced replacement tissues. Damage done by degenerative disorders like diabetes, Parkinson's disease or Alzheimer's disease might be reversed. Biologists might be able to create organs for transplant using merely a dead skin cell.

Ethical implications involved in human cloning are only temporary. This can be shown in the development of In Vitro Fertilisation (IVF). During the 1960s and 1970s, opponents of IVF argued that it was unsafe, children would be deformed, American families would be destroyed or changed, and it was against God's will. These are the same arguments being used against human cloning. Eighty-five per cent of Americans thought IVF should be outlawed during the 1970s. Public opinion changed when they saw Louie Brown, the first child born using IVF. People noticed that he was just a child. Their fears of IVF subsided. It became a routine medical procedure within a few years. This will most likely be the case with human cloning.

Many of the ethical arguments against human cloning are induced by misconception. The 'Mini-Hitler' scenario I've listed above is far-fetched, but that is exactly the kind of thing people think about when they hear the word 'cloning'. People think that cloning technology can produce an exact copy of an existing adult human being. This isn't true. Cloning technology can only produce a cloned embryo. The embryo must develop in a uterus. The developed child must experience childhood and adolescence. People think that a clone will be both behaviourally and physically identical to its donor. This also isn't true. The clone will probably be identical physically, but not behaviorally. Genes contribute to the array of our abilities and limits, but our behaviour and mentality are constantly shaped by environmental factors. Even identical twins show differences in behavioural and mental characteristics. Someone trying to clone a future Adolf Hitler might instead produce a modestly talented painter. Ethicists are afraid that a subordinate class of humans will be created as tissue and organ donors. They are afraid that the rights of these clones will be violated. These fears are outrageous and ridiculous. These ethicists have been the victims of misconception. Cloned humans could no more be 'harvested' for their organs than people can be today.

Many of the ethical arguments against human cloning are induced by misconception

Another ethical dilemma is the psychological well-being of the cloned child. People wonder what kind of a relationship a cloned child will have with his/her parent that is physically identical. They are curious as to how the child will deal with the pressure of constantly being compared to an esteemed or beloved person who has already lived. We need to remember that the single most important factor affecting the quality of a child's life is the love and devotion he/she receives from parents, not the methods or circumstances of the person's birth. Since children produced by cloning will probably be extremely wanted children, there is no reason to think that with good counselling support for their parents they will not experience the love and care they deserve. What will life be like for the first generation of cloned children? Being at the centre of scientific and popular attention will not be easy for them. They and their parents will also have to negotiate the worrisome problems created by genetic identity and unavoidable expectations. However, there may also be some novel satisfactions. As cross-generational twins, a cloned child and his/her parent may experience some of the unique intimacy now shared by sibling twins.

Animal research will eventually indicate that human cloning can be done at no greater physical risk to the child than IVF posed when it was first introduced. It would be better if such research would be done openly in the US, Canada, Europe or Japan. Established government agencies could provide careful oversight of the implications of the studies for human subjects. The most probable way that it will happen will be, if not yet already, in a clandestine fashion. A couple desperate for a child will put their hopes in the hands of a researcher seeking fame. Advanced Cell Technologies (ACT) have already created the first human embryo. They took DNA from a man's leg and injected it into a cow's egg with its nucleus removed. There have also been reports of similar work in South Korea. Someone is going to clone a human with or without government assistance. It would be beneficial if our federal government regulated such experiments, rather than outlaw them. Outlawing something will not necessarily stop it from happening. Regulating human cloning will allow our federal government to closely overlook experiments pertaining to human cloning.

The federal government should regulate human cloning. Banning it would deprive many people of beneficial treatment they need. I have mentioned only a few of cloning technology's significant benefits. Cloning technology can lead to a better understanding of cell differentiation. This would allow biologists to produce tissues and organs for transplant. Cloning can help carriers of genetic defects to have healthy children. It can even help to completely eradicate genetic mutations and defects. Treatment of infertility is one of its most promising benefits. Cloning technology can help infertile people to have their own children, one of life's most powerful biological drives. Besides, ethical implications involved in human cloning are only temporary. They are induced by misconception. Education will change people's negative attitude towards human cloning. If we give human cloning a chance, it will most likely become a part of our daily lives.

■ The above information is from the Human Cloning Foundation's website: www.humancloning.org

Stem cell research

Information from the Human Fertilisation & Embryology Authority (HFEA)

Stem cells reproduce indefinitely and have the capacity to develop (differentiate) into various different cell types. They have potential to treat a wide range of serious, but common, diseases like diabetes, Parkinson's and certain types of heart disease. These diseases are a major cause of illness and death and, for many of them, no effective treatment currently exists. At present the most widely used stem cell-based therapy is bone marrow transplant for leukaemia. Future regenerative therapies could transplant stem cells into diseased or damaged tissue to repair patient's organs. There are a number of different ways of making stem cells for treatment. They fall basically into two sorts: embryonic and adult.

Embryonic stem cells vs. adult stem cells

Although adult stem cells are found in many parts of the human body, embryonic stem cells have proven to be more flexible. Embryonic stem cells have the potential to develop into a wide range of tissue types and are called 'pluripotent'. This is why research is done on embryonic stem cells.

UK Stem Cell Bank

The UK Stem Cell Bank was launched by the Medical Research Council (MRC) in September 2002. The bank will be a vital resource to support the advance of research into stem cells. It is the world's first stem cell bank of its type. The bank exists to establish fully characterised and quality-controlled cell banks. These will be supplied to accredited scientific research teams and eventually pharmaceutical companies, to enable the development of broad-ranging cell therapies. The UK Stem Cell Bank is based at the National Institute for Biological Standards and Control (NIBSC).

Legislation

The HFEA is responsible for controlling the creation and use in research of embryos up to 14 days. This includes research which may generate embryonic stem cells. All embryo research, whether publicly or privately funded, must be approved by the HFEA and it is unlawful in this country for embryonic stem cells to be generated without a licence from the HFEA.

In January 2001, Parliament agreed to allow research for therapeutic purposes on cells derived from human embryos. (Human Fertilisation and Embryology (Research Purposes) Regulations 2001.)

The three additional (therapeutic) purposes are:

- Increasing knowledge about the development of embryos
- Increasing knowledge about serious disease
- Enabling any such knowledge to be applied in developing treatments for serious disease

As part of this agreement, a House of Lords Select committee on Stem Cell Research was formed to examine the issues in more detail.

The Human Reproductive Cloning Act 2001 came into place in December 2001. The Act 'prohibits the placing in a woman of a human embryo which has been created otherwise than by fertilisation'. This act made it clear that methods such as Cell Nuclear Replacement (CNR) could be used as a research tool to enable therapies to be developed, without the concern that embryos might be created for reproductive cloning.

Embryonic stem cells have the potential to develop into a wide range of tissue types

■ The above information is from the Human Fertilisation & Embryology Authority's website: www.hfea.gov.uk

European attitudes to six applications of biotechnology in 2002

Contrary to what might be expected, the term 'cloning' does not lead to automatic rejection. When cloning is employed in an application that is seen to be useful, people are prepared to discount the risks and affirm support.

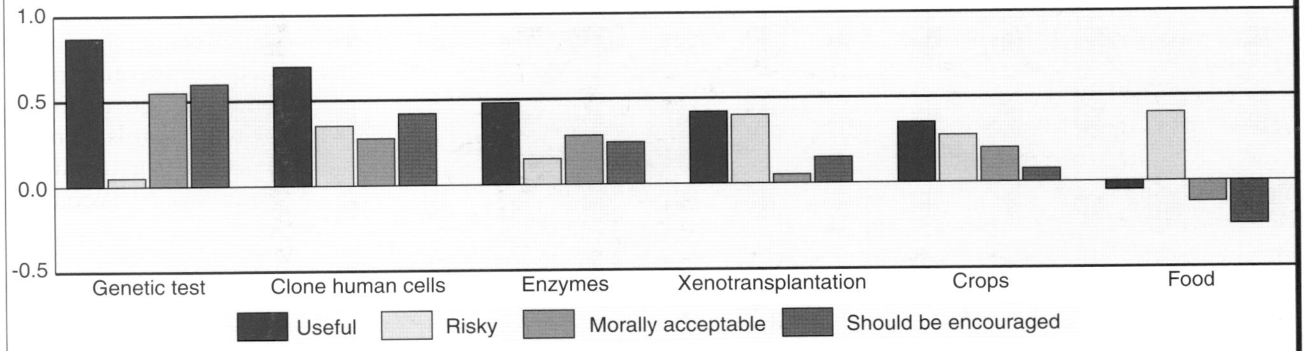

1.0
0.5
0.0
-0.5
Genetic test
Clone human cells
Enzymes
Xenotransplantation
Crops
Food
Useful
Risky
Morally acceptable
Should be encouraged

Source: Europeans and Biotechology in 2002, European Opinion Research Group

Cloned human embryos are stem cell breakthrough

Scientists have demonstrated for the first time that therapeutic cloning in humans can be achieved.

The researchers in South Korea created 30 cloned embryos that grew to about 100 cells in size – further than any verified experiment so far. This meant they were able to harvest embryonic stem cells from one of the embryos. They further showed that the ESCs could develop into a variety of tissue types.

Their long-term hope is that such a procedure would provide a source of perfectly matched transplant tissue for the treatment of diseases such as diabetes and Parkinson's.

'In this precise moment there is a person in South Korea walking around with [embryonic] stem cells tailor-made for her,' says Jose Cibelli from Michigan State University. He is the only US researcher involved with the work, although not the cloning experiments themselves.

'It is a great piece of work,' Cibelli says. All the experts contacted by *New Scientist* agreed, praising the experiments as remarkable. Cloning in primates has been regarded as especially challenging and perhaps even impossible.

Proof of principle

However, several scientists expressed concern that the proof of principle now published by the Koreans might assist maverick scientists in attempting to clone a baby. The scientific consensus is that this would be far too risky.

'Now that the methodology is publicly available it's time to enact a ban on cloning for reproductive purposes,' says Robert Lanza from Advanced Cell Technology in Massachusetts, the company that published the first account of a cloned human embryo in 2001.

The vast majority of nations support a global ban on cloning babies, but attempts at the United Nations to implement one have stalled. This is because some countries, including the US, want therapeutic cloning banned too, as it involves the destruction of embryos.

Chemical key

The key difficulty researchers had anticipated in cloning humans or other primates relates to chemical factors that assist cell division.

Unlike eggs from other species, primate eggs have cell division factors that are lost when the nucleus is removed from the egg – the first step of cloning. Some scientists argued that this would doom any chance of yielding healthy embryos.

But now Woo Suk Hwang, from Seoul National University, and his colleagues have shown for the first time that, even though the process remains inefficient, cloning in humans can in fact be attained.

'This is a spectacular discovery. This group deserves tremendous credit for this heroic achievement,' says Gerald Schatten, director of the Pittsburgh Development Center at the Magee-Womens Research Institute. His team had published a widely cited article arguing that primates would be extremely hard to clone.

Double donor

For their experiments, the Korean scientists used 242 eggs donated from 16 healthy women. Each woman was the donor of both the egg and the cell from which the nucleus was taken, before being placed into the egg.

About a quarter of the treated eggs developed into blastocysts, the stage from which ESCs can be harvested. According to the authors, the rates compare well with those in cow and pig cloning.

However, of the 30 blastocysts cultured, only one yielded a cell line of ESCs. The team cannot explain this low efficiency, though they speculate that perhaps many of the failed embryos had chromosomal abnormalities.

The stem cell line derived from the cloned embryo had many of the characteristics of ESCs, including an ability to divide indefinitely. When injected into mice, they formed several tissue types including cartilage, muscle and bone.

So why did cloning work for the South Koreans? Nobody knows the answer yet, but techniques such as using a much gentler method to extract the cells' nuclei may have helped.

At this early stage, and with unanswered questions about the safety of using ESCs for therapy, Cibelli warns that it will be many years before medical treatments are developed: 'We have so much to do before putting this into patients.'

■ This article first appeared in *The New Scientist*.

Why is using stem cells controversial?

The ethical issues

Few people express concern about the use in research of cells or tissues taken from an adult with his or her informed consent or from cord blood taken with the consent of the mother. However, the status and use of human embryos in research are more controversial.

Why is using stem cells controversial?

A significant minority of people believe that the use of any embryo for research purposes is unethical and unacceptable on the grounds that an embryo is a human being entitled to full human status from the moment of conception. Pro-life groups and some religions argue that such research should be banned. For more information see the House of Lords select committee report.

The UK's present law, which permits embryo research under strict controls, has evolved over nearly twenty years of public and Parliamentary debate beginning with the Committee of Enquiry chaired by Baroness Warnock from 1982 to 1984. Whilst protection of the embryo is deemed important, successive Governments have taken the position that embryo research intended to bring benefits for many is ethically acceptable.

Recent scientific progress with adult stem cell research has fuelled this debate. Peter Garrett, Director of Research for LIFE (a leading pro-life charity and lobbying group), argues that adult stem cell research makes embryonic cloning as unnecessary as it is unethical.

The Government's position remains that it is important to pursue all areas of stem cell research responsibly, ethically and to a high scientific standard, in order to find treatment for disease as early as possible.

Can humans be cloned?

There has also been concern about the likelihood of 'designer' babies or the creation of a genetic sub-class. Wilder predictions include cloning dead people and people seeking eternal life by cloning themselves.

Using cell nuclear replacement for the purpose of reproductive cloning was made illegal in December 2001 when the Government introduced the Human Reproductive Cloning Act. The Act carries a ten-year jail sentence for anyone attempting to create a child using the cell nuclear replacement technique.

Mainstream scientists are against the idea of human cloning, and the Human Fertilisation and Embryology Authority regulates all research on embryos, thus ensuring that human cloning will never take place

Mainstream scientists are against the idea of human cloning, and the Human Fertilisation and Embryology Authority regulates all research on embryos, thus ensuring that human cloning will never take place.

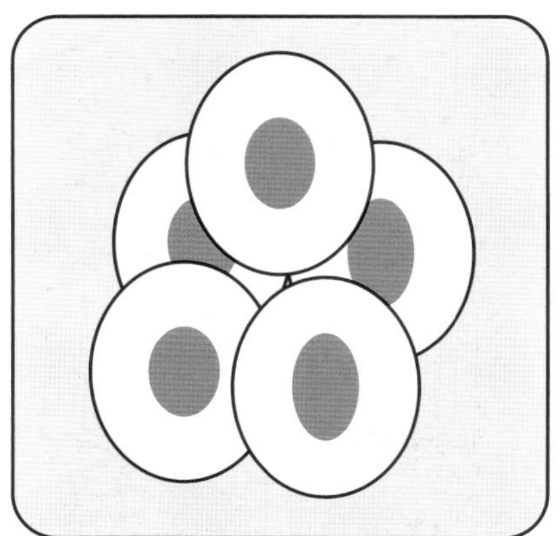

Aside from the ethical considerations, the risks involved in the cell nuclear technique are far too great. It took 277 attempts to clone Dolly (see below). Human cloning would result in a large number of miscarriages and deformities before a human could be successfully cloned. The long-term health risks are unknown.

Animal cloning

In 1997, scientists at the Roslin Institute in Edinburgh announced that they had successfully cloned a mammal using cell nuclear replacement.

Dolly was the first mammal cloned from a cell from an adult animal. She was derived from cells that had been taken from the udder of a six-year-old Finn Dorset ewe and cultured for several weeks in the laboratory. Individual cells were then fused with unfertilised eggs from which the genetic material had been removed.

Two hundred and seventy-seven of these reconstructed eggs – each now with a diploid nucleus from the adult animal – were cultured for six days in temporary recipients.

Twenty-nine of the eggs that appeared to have developed normally to the blastocyst stage were implanted into surrogate Scottish Blackface ewes. One gave rise to live lamb, Dolly, some 148 days later.

Dolly was put to sleep by vets on 14 February 2003 at the age of seven years. She died from causes believed to be unrelated to cloning.

■ The above information is from the Department of Health's website: www.dh.gov.uk

First stem cell bank opens in UK

The world's first Stem Cell Bank opened in the UK 19 May 2004. Under the controversial new project embryonic stem cells will be stored at the Bank and used for research into degenerative diseases such as Parkinson's, Alzheimer's and diabetes.

Britain's first two lines of human embryonic stem cells have been deposited as Health Minister Lord Warner declared the facility open.

They were developed separately by researchers at King's College London and the Centre for Life in Newcastle.

The £2.6 million bank, the first of its kind in the world, is housed at the National Institute for Biological Standards and Control in Potters Bar, Hertfordshire.

Scientists hope in future it will drive research into revolutionary new ways of treating incurable and degenerative diseases such as Parkinson's, Alzheimer's and diabetes.

Stem cells are 'master' cells that can be made to develop into different types of tissue.

Embryonic stem cells, extracted from pinhead-sized undeveloped embryos, are unique in that they have the potential to become any kind of tissue in the body, including muscle, bone, nerves and organs.

Replacement tissue

It is hoped stem cells can be used to grow replacement tissue for damaged parts of the body.

They might, for instance, be used to create 'spare part' brain neurons or heart muscle.

Cell lines derived from stem cells can continue to multiply and reproduce themselves indefinitely. Those held at the Stem Cell Bank will grow into a vast reservoir of cells that can be used for research and ultimately treatment.

Although the Government has given the green light to research involving embryonic stem cells, their use is controversial and opposed by some on ethical grounds.

The Bank will also hold stem cells derived from foetal and adult tissues. Applications to deposit stem cells or access banked cell lines will be reviewed and authorised by a high level Steering Committee chaired by Lord Naren Patel.

Lord Warner said: 'This Bank is the first of its kind in the world and confirms the UK's position as a leader in stem cell research.

'This potentially revolutionary research could benefit thousands of patients whose lives are blighted by devastating diseases such as Parkinson's, stroke and Alzheimer's.

'Today's launch is further evidence of the Government's commitment to strengthen research and development so that NHS patients can reap the full benefits of the latest advances in science.'

Incurable diseases

The Bank is funded by the Medical Research Council (MRC) and the Biotechnology and Biological Sciences Research Council (BBSRC).

Professor Colin Blakemore, Chief Executive of the MRC, said: 'Stem cell research offers real promise for the treatment of currently incurable diseases. The Bank will ensure that researchers can explore the enormous potential of this exciting science for the future benefit of patients.'

Embryonic stem cells cultured by the King's College scientists were obtained as a by-product of In-Vitro Fertilisation treatment and pre-implantation genetic diagnosis (PGD).

Theirs was one of the first two laboratories in the UK to be granted a licence to generate human embryonic stem (hES) cell lines.

Currently, only a handful of hES lines exist worldwide. They vary in quality, and access to them for research can be expensive and limited.

Dr Stephen Minger, head of the Stem Cell Laboratory at King's College, said: 'The stem cells we are banking will be a crucial resource for future research into diseases such as Type 1 diabetes, Parkinson's and Alzheimer's.

'The Bank accepts only high quality lines that will be of benefit to other scientists, and we are delighted our cells are among the first to be accepted.'

Professor Peter Braude, clinical head of the Preimplantation Genetic Programme at Guy's and St Thomas's Hospital in London, said: 'We are very grateful to our patients for rising to this need to help us develop a national resource for research and therapy.

'We feel privileged that they have done this comfortable in the knowledge that their contribution has not jeopardised their own fertility or genetic treatment in any way.'

Pro-life charity LIFE said it was opposed to the new stem cell bank, adding that using human embryos as a tissue source was 'unethical, unnecessary and dangerous'.

■ This article first appeared in *The Daily Mail*, 19 May 2004.

Therapeutic or biomedical cloning

Information from the Association of the British Pharmaceutical Industry

This technique is also known as somatic cell nuclear transfer or research cloning. Scientists are keen to remove the link in the public mind between this developing technique and adult cell cloning, because the intention in therapeutic cloning is NOT to produce a new animal or plant. The hope instead is to produce pluripotent stem cells which can in turn develop into new tissues or organs for people who are seriously ill.

So many people suffer severe disability and even die because various parts of their body stop working properly. From the sugar-balance problems of diabetes to the tremor, rigidity and loss of control of Parkinson's disease; from the life-threatening shock of a heart attack to the horror of paralysis due to spinal injuries, there are literally millions of people who could benefit if it was possible to replace body parts which no longer work properly.

Therapeutic cloning involves using cells from an individual to produce a cloned early embryo which is then used as a source of embryonic stem cells. As it becomes possible to control the development of these stem cells into specific cell types, tissues and organs, it should be possible to grow new nerve cells, muscle cells and even new kidneys and hearts for people who desperately need them. What is more, because the patient donates the original adult cells, there will be a perfect DNA match with the new healthy tissue when it is introduced – so there will be no rejection problems.

An adult cell is taken from the patient and the nucleus is removed. At the same time the nucleus is taken out of a donated ovum, and the adult cell nucleus and the empty ovum are combined. A mild electric shock stimulates embryonic development to begin. Once a ball of cells has

developed, as many embryonic stem cells as possible are harvested, destroying the embryo. The harvested stem cells can then be stimulated to produce whatever tissue is needed.

This technique still needs a great deal of development, not least because scientists have still not unravelled the secrets of directing stem cells to form exactly the tissue they want. Therapeutic cloning seems to have enormous medical potential, but there are many ethical issues surrounding it – not least because it involves the use of human ova and the formation of an early embryo which is then destroyed.

■ The above information is from the Association of the British Pharmaceutical Industry's Schools website which can be found at www.abpischools.org.uk

Therapeutic or biomedical cloning

Also known as somatic cell nuclear transfer or research cloning, the idea is not to produce a new animal or plant. The hope is to produce new tissues or organs for people who are seriously ill with problems ranging from diabetes and Parkinson's disease to heart attacks and spinal injuries. The technique still needs a lot of development, but the medical potential is enormous.

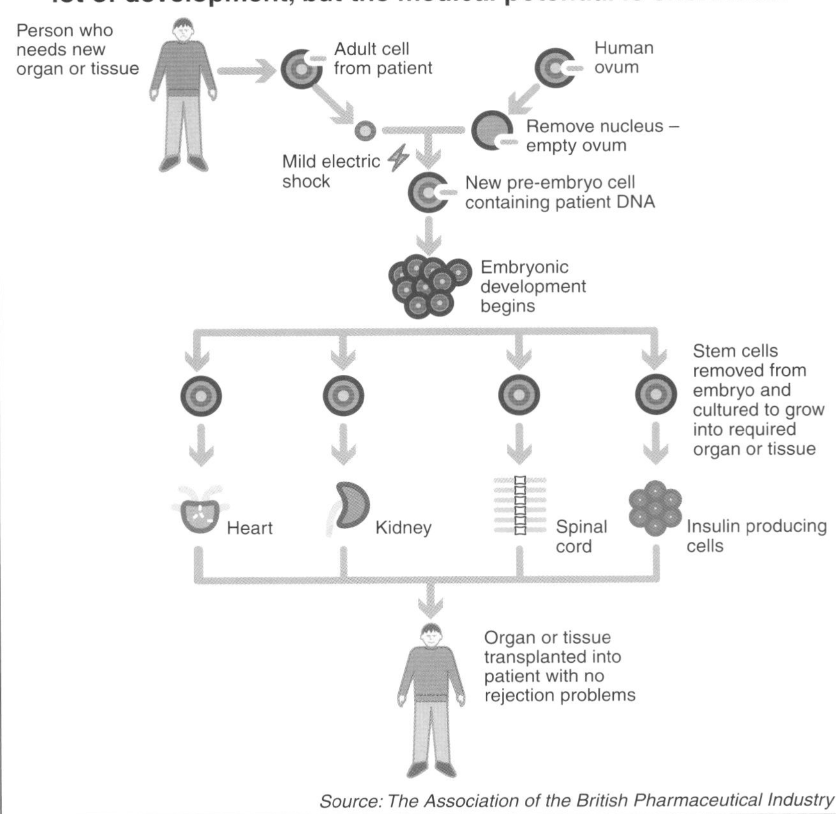

Source: The Association of the British Pharmaceutical Industry

Korean clones – unsafe, unnecessary and unethical

By Peter Saunders

The February 2004 announcement[1] that South Korean scientists had cloned 30 human embryos generated the media frenzy and overhyped predictions we have come to expect in this area of research. But the true facts were less impressive.

The team at Seoul National University used 242 eggs from 16 women donors; from which they derived 30 blastocysts. They ended up with just one line of stem cells, derived from a blastocyst made from an enucleated egg and transplanted nuclear material from the same woman.[2] The theoretical possibility of producing stem cells for therapeutic purposes from cloned embryos has thus moved one step closer but many practical difficulties remain.

First, the low efficiency of mammalian cloning (only 0-5% become viable offspring)[3] highlights the high frequency of genetic abnormalities resulting from the technology. It is not yet known whether similar abnormalities would occur in stem cells derived from cloned embryos, but it stands to reason that they would. Second, some of the diseases given as candidates for cell therapy are autoimmune conditions like type I diabetes; suggesting that cloned stem cells derived from the patient would induce the same rejection when transplanted and thus be ineffective. Third there remain concerns, based on the difficulty of controlling the growth of transplanted fetal cells, about embryonic stem cells functioning abnormally after transfer.

These concerns about the likely effectiveness and safety of therapeutic cloning have not been truthfully conveyed to a public fed on 20-second soundbites which fail to do justice to the scientific facts or complex ethical issues involved.

Even if the practical difficulties are overcome, the key ethical objection remains. The end of saving life cannot ever justify the means of creating and cannibalising human embryos, cloned or otherwise. Furthermore, allowing such research at all will lead inevitably to attempts to produce reproductive clones, as long as rogue scientists exist. And meanwhile, huge advances in the ethical alternative of adult stem cell technology continue to make embryo cloning rapidly redundant.

The end of saving life cannot ever justify the means of creating and cannibalising human embryos, cloned or otherwise

It is very sad that the British media and public have been consistently misled into seeing cloned embryos as a panacea for treating diseases like Parkinson's and Alzheimer's, through the Government's failure to highlight the dangers and to rectify misconceptions about the properties of adult stem cells propagated in the now seriously dated 2000 Donaldson report *Stem Cell Research*.

Selective interpretation and presentation of scientific data is both irresponsible and dangerous because it falsely raises the hopes of vulnerable people. Honest and balanced reporting of the facts should always take precedence over the prestige and profit motives of the British government and biotech industry.

Cloning and cannibalising embryos for stem cells in the way that the Korean scientists have is unsafe, unnecessary and unethical. A gullible and ill-informed public needs to be better informed of the dangers and made more aware of safer ethical alternatives for developing treatments for people with degenerative diseases.

References

1. www.sciencemag.org/cgi/content/abstract/1094515
2. Radford T. Korean Scientists clone 30 embryos. *BMJ* 2004; 328:421 (21 February)
3. Wilmut I. Are there any normal cloned mammals? *Nature Med* 2002; 8:215-6

■ The above information is from the Christian Medical Fellowship's Ethics for Schools website: www.ethicsforschools.org

Cloned embryo research poses ethical problems

By Dr Bruce

The first cloned human embryos were announced by Korean scientists in early 2004. Two UK proposals for research involving cloned embryos to create stem cells have also received prominent media coverage. One is from the Newcastle Fertility Centre; the other is expected from Professor Ian Wilmut's group at the Roslin Institute. Such research is formally legal in the UK but ethically controversial. The European Commission's ethical advisory group considered it premature and the European Parliament has voted against it. We evaluate some of the ethical issues involved.

Link to reproductive cloning

The stated aim of the Newcastle proposal is to improve the efficiency of making cloned human embryos for stem cell research. However, it seems unwise to allow research which would make it easier for maverick scientists to make and implant cloned embryos to create cloned babies, regardless of major risks and ethical objections, in some other country where there was little or no regulation. The UK bears a moral responsibility to the wider international community for the outcomes of its actions here. Given that Parliament overwhelmingly outlawed reproductive human cloning, the UK should refuse cloned embryo research applications until there has at least been a United Nations agreement to ban reproductive human cloning. The Church of Scotland had called for such a ban in 1997. A French and German proposal is currently stalled at the UN.

Therapeutic cloning

The Newcastle group gives a justification that their research could eventually lead to so-called 'therapeutic' cloning for degenerative diseases. Cloned embryos would be created from a patient's own cells to make replacement cells that are genetically matched, to avoid the possibility of rejection of cells derived from IVF embryos. This is seriously in doubt because of the impracticability of donating millions of human eggs to treat hundreds of thousands of UK sufferers of the range of degenerative diseases for which therapeutic cloning claims are made. Ian Wilmut has stated that 'it is unlikely to be practical for routine use'. This means that, despite the claims, therapeutic cloning would not be a medical breakthrough for humanity as a whole but only a technique for those rich enough to afford it. The ethical advisory board of the Geron Corporation which funded some of Roslin's stem cell research raised this issue, which remains unresolved. The case for cloned embryo research for therapy is thus dubious, compared with using stem cells from more readily available spare IVF embryos.

Some have suggested making cloned embryos from human cells and cow eggs. This raises as many ethical problems as it might solve. The Chief Medical Officer's committee of 2000 recommended 'The mixing of human adult (somatic) cells with the live eggs of any animal species should not be permitted.' This view was endorsed by the UK Government who promised primary legislation and 'calls upon bodies funding research to make it to clear that they will not fund or support research involving the creation of such hybrids'.

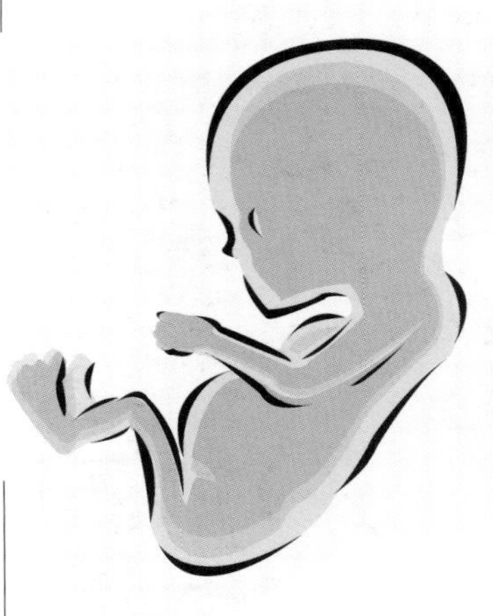

Cloning embryos for research

The real scientific focus of the two proposals is, however, not therapeutic cloning as normally conceived. It is to use cloning technology to make disease state cells – to study motor neurone disease in the Roslin proposal, and diabetes in the Newcastle case. Cloned embryos would be created from a patient's cells, and stem cells taken from them to generate a continuous supply of the diseased cells. A House of Lords select committee concluded that cloned embryos 'should not be created for research purposes unless there is a demonstrable and exceptional need which cannot be met by the use of surplus embryos'. Speculative research is not enough justification. Are these exceptional cases? They require a careful medical evaluation of the realistic expectations by comparison with other options. We should not resort to the drastic step of creating cloned human embryos unless it would achieve a major medical breakthrough that nothing else could hope to achieve, and that is by no means clear thus far.

■ Dr Bruce is Director of the Society, Religion and Technology Project of the Church of Scotland, which has been in the forefront to the debate on animal and human cloning since 1996. For further information visit their website: www.srtp.org.uk

Cloning and stem cells

Frequently asked questions

Is cloning 'unnatural'?

Not at all – some organisms in nature only reproduce using cloning – not only bacteria and yeasts, but also larger organisms like some snails and shrimp. Because in nature sexual reproduction is the only way to improve the genetic stock of a species, most asexual species tend to die off, but at least one – a shrimp called *Artemia perthenogenetica* – has survived for at least 30 million years. Many more species, including the aphid, reproduce by cloning most of the time, only reproducing sexually every few generations. Perhaps one day humankind may follow their lead.

Is an identical twin essentially the same as a clone?

Only if the clone is born at the same time from the same womb as its clone, as we now know that what a fetus is exposed to in the womb, in the way of nutrition or alcohol or drugs or perhaps even stress hormones, can influence its physical and mental development.

Could some lunatic clone Hitler if human cloning were perfected?

Just possibly – but they wouldn't get what they wanted. First, they would need some living cells from his body – unless it was frozen or otherwise preserved soon after death they would probably be unusable. More importantly, because of differences in the environment of the womb and upbringing clone Hitlers would not act, think or even necessarily look like the original.

Could clones be 'farmed' to provide spare body parts for their 'parent' clone without problems of tissue rejection?

Possibly, although we don't know enough yet to be confident that rejection would be eliminated entirely. You would also have to wait a number of years until the clone's organs were mature enough to transplant, and of course your actions would be highly illegal unless your clone was willing to act as a donor as a clone would be just as human as you or I. Even leaving aside the ethical concerns, with the progress that is being made in understanding and coping with tissue rejection, you would be more likely to have a pig's heart in your future than a clone's.

Would a clone have a soul?

Though we are not theologians if you grant souls to identical twins and to the various kinds of 'test tube babies' already being born then it follows that a clone would have one too.

Could people be cloned without conscious brains (so their body parts could be harvested with fewer moral qualms)?

No. For starters, whatever consciousness is, it doesn't reside in any one brain structure or set of genes that could be easily removed from the clone before or during its development. Moreover, attempting to surgically or genetically erase someone's 'consciousness' is itself morally dubious. It would also be hard to know if your 'technique' worked. A person can look and behave like a mindless vegetable but have a very active mind – witness the paralysed French writer, Jean-Dominique Bauby, who dictated a 130-page novel by moving an eyelid.

Could vital organs be grown using cloning without the rest of a body?

Possibly – but nobody is even close to knowing how. Contrary to scientists' expectations, the birth of Dolly shows it is possible to reprogramme the cell of an adult (or at least its genome) so that it begins development all over again. This newly discovered flexibility means it may one day be possible to reprogramme skin or blood cells so that they grow into 'spare part' tissues and organs, rather than whole organisms. But the technical obstacles will be huge.

Could cloning be used to create 'super warriors' or super-intelligent people?

Possibly – though we don't yet know enough about human genetics to do much 'improving' of people. So far, because of ethical concerns, geneticists are concentrating on finding the causes of genetic diseases and then curing them. Cloning makes it easier to meddle with human and animal genes but is not necessarily genetic improvement, by itself. Even before recent discoveries a considerable amount of genetic improvement of animals was already taking place. A thoroughbred horse is essentially genetically engineered, for example.

Genetic engineering is rather a hit and miss technique. You try to add the gene you want in the right place, in the right cell, and sometimes that works. Before cloning, genetically engineering a sheep, for example, might have involved injecting DNA into the egg or early embryo. It was only once the animal grew up and was tested that it was possible to see if the desired genetic change had been introduced and stably incorporated into the animal's germline.

Cloning, in theory, allows you to turn any cell into an animal. So instead of injecting DNA into an egg, you can shoot DNA into cells in a petri dish, allow them to grow and look among millions of cells for the type of genetic alteration you want. Since it is so much easier to manipulate cells than sheep – not to mention the fact that it is easier to feed, say, 100,000 cells than the same number of livestock – much rarer and more subtle gene manipulation can be accomplished, such as replacing one gene for another, or changing a single DNA letter of a gene.

Once you have cells with the desired genetic character, they are fused with an egg from which the chromosomes have been removed. Any animal that grows up from that experiment will have the genetic change in every cell of their body.

Could cloning be used to save endangered species?

At the moment its success rate is very low (Dolly was only cloned after 276 tries) but if this can be improved on it might well turn out to be useful to increase the population of hard-to-breed animals. Extinct animals (or animals without females) would be more difficult. A female can't normally give birth to an animal of a different species, although in certain cases a female of a closely-related species could give birth to a clone of a different species (see the example of Noah the gaur).

Could cloning help gay couples to conceive and make men unneccessary for procreation?

In principle, yes. Of course a clone would have to be the identical twin of one or the other partner – it would be difficult to duplicate any of the mixing of genes that occurs during sexual reproduction using cloning techniques.

■ This article first appeared in *The New Scientist*.

Milestones in UK stem cell related research and regulation

1973: Isolation of mouse embryonic stem cells by Cambridge scientists.

1978: Following fertilisation of animal and human eggs outside of the body by Cambridge scientists, first IVF baby born.

1982: Formation of the Warnock Committee to examine the moral questions surrounding assisted reproduction and embryo research.

1984: Warnock Report endorses human embryo research into reproductive-related areas but advises tight regulation.

1990: Human Fertilisation and Embryology Act passed by both Houses of Parliament. Human Fertilisation and Embryology Authority (HFEA) designated statutory body to enforce provisions of legislation and established in 1991.

1996: A sheep is cloned by cell nuclear replacement (CNR) techniques at Roslin Institute in Edinburgh.

1998: HFEA and Human Genetics Advisory Commission working party recommends that CNR be investigated for therapeutic purposes but not for reproductive cloning.

2000: Report by Donaldson Commission, chaired by Chief Medical Officer Sir Liam Donaldson, recommends that research using human embryos (created by IVF or CNR) to increase understanding of human disease and disorders and their cell-based treatments should be permitted subject to controls in the 1990 HFE Act. Also that the Research Councils should be encouraged to establish a programme of stem cell research and consider the feasibility of establishing collections of stem cells for research use.

2001: Human Fertilisation and Embryology (Research Purposes) Regulations 2001 designed to implement the recommendations of the Donaldson Commission passed by Parliament; three new purposes added to the 1990 Act. House of Lords appoints a select committee to examine the issues arising from the new regulations, including those of human cloning and stem cell research. Parliament introduces additional legislation prohibiting reproductive cloning.

2002: House of Lords Select Committee concludes that stem cells have great therapeutic potential and that research should be conducted on both adult and embryonic stem cells. Also that a stem cell bank should be established and overseen by a steering committee.

2002: The UK Stem Cell Bank, funded by the Medical Research Council and the Biotechnology and Biological Sciences Research Council, established at the National Institute for Biological Standards and Control. This bank to be a repository for stem cells derived from adult, fetal and embryonic tissues and to be open to academics and industrialists from the UK and abroad. Steering committee established to oversee the bank and the use of stem cell lines and to develop codes of practice.

2003: Researchers at King's College London generate the UK's first embryonic stem cell line.

■ The above information is taken from an issue of *LabNotes*: New Biology and Society, Stem cells: Potent Research. *LabNotes* is a free resource for schools produced by the Wellcome Trust independent biomedical research charity.

Human embryo research plan is first of its kind

By Ian Sample, Science Correspondent

Members of the Human Fertilisation and Embryology Authority met 17 June 2004 to consider the first application to clone human embryos.

If it is approved, the team of researchers at Newcastle University, led by Dr Miodrag Stojkovic, will clone human embryos and use them as sources of embryonic stem cells, which have the potential to form any of the hundreds of different tissues found in the body. The researchers hope their work will lead to huge advances in medicine, among them novel treatments for disease.

'Our aim is clear: to use these stem cells to find a solution to diabetes,' said Dr Stojkovic, at the university's institute for human genetics.

Many scientists believe embryonic stem cell research could usher in cures for conditions as diverse as Parkinson's disease, Alzheimer's and motor neurone disease. But critics called on the HFEA to reject the application, calling the research unethical, unnecessary and dangerous.

Cloning human embryos to make babies is outlawed in Britain, but so-called therapeutic cloning, where embryos are created for research, was made legal under strict guidelines in 2002.

While the HFEA's research licence committee met 17 June 2004 to discuss the application, a spokeswoman for the authority said their decision was not expected to be announced until the next week.

The HFEA can grant licences for research on embryos only if the work meets at least one of three tests: that it will increase our understanding of how embryos develop, improve our knowledge of serious disease, or enable the development of treatments for serious disease. Embryos created for research must be destroyed before they are 14 days old, when they are a ball of cells no larger than a pinhead.

The HFEA has already studied the scientists' CVs, sent the team's application to leading academics for comment and carried out an inspection of the labs where the research might take place.

If the HFEA approves the application, as many scientists expect, Dr Stojkovic's group plans to take unfertilised eggs, which would otherwise be discarded as surplus from IVF clinics, and remove the genetic material inside them. The hollowed-out eggs will then be filled with genetic material taken from the skin cells of diabetics.

Cloning human embryos to make babies is outlawed in Britain, but so-called therapeutic cloning was made legal under strict guidelines in 2002

Nurturing the eggs for six to eight days produces a tiny ball of around 100 cells, from which embryonic stem cells can be extracted. By treating the stem cells with various growth promoters, Dr Stojkovic plans to turn the stem cells into pancreas cells.

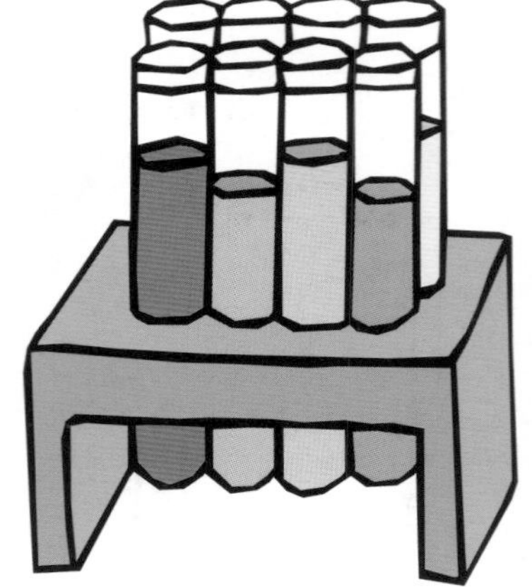

Because they are genetically identical to the other cells in the person's body, the newly created pancreas cells can be implanted without being rejected by the immune system. Once there, they should start producing insulin, potentially curing the condition.

The push to begin research on cloned human embryos has reignited a storm over the necessity, ethics and safety of therapeutic cloning.

Patrick Cusworth, of the anti-abortion group Life, said: 'This is a profoundly dehumanising process. It attempts to change the status of the human embryo as the beginning point of human life into little more than a pharmaceutical product.

'It's also giving diabetics false hopes. You would need around 35m human eggs to treat everyone in the UK with diabetes. It's totally unfeasible.'

Others added their voices to the protests. 'This research is a waste of public money, and crosses important ethical lines for the first time. It is very unlikely to produce anything medically useful,' said David King, of the pressure group Human Genetics Alert. 'We don't believe that embryos are people with rights to life, but neither is it right to create them as raw material for research. It is vital that this receives wide public debate, and that we do not get stuck in the sterile pro-life versus science opposition.'

Dr King criticised the HFEA, suggesting approval of the research was likely for political reasons.

'It's very clear that the scientific community is very nervous that the UN could pass a treaty banning so-called therapeutic cloning around the world, so they're trying to convince UN delegates that it's worthwhile research by getting some of these research programmes up and running. That way, they could say that by introducing a broad ban, the UN would be shutting down something that'll be a great benefit to humanity.'

The UN is due to consider the case for therapeutic cloning in November 2004.

Some critics fear that if the research is approved, scientific results from the Newcastle group could give vital clues to maverick scientists intent on using similar techniques to create cloned human babies. But Dr Stojkovic said the information on how to clone embryos was already in the public domain. Earlier this year, scientists in South Korea announced they had produced the first cloned human embryos.

'I completely understand the ethical objections, but we are using eggs that are surplus to IVF treatment, which failed to be fertilised,' said Dr Stojkovic. 'Instead of being thrown away they have been donated for research. The way I think of it is, why put something in the rubbish bin when it can be used in such a valuable way?

Embryo cloning

Individual cells are taken from an early embryo and encouraged to develop into more identical embryos – it is a form of artificial twinning. This technique is used to make lots of identical copies of original embryos which have been genetically modified to produce human proteins. The adult animals which result provide life-saving treatments for thousands of people.

Early embryo (cluster of identical cells)

Cells separated

Each cell develops into an identical embryo

Each embryo is implanted into a different surrogate mother

Identical cloned offspring born

Source: The Association of the British Pharmaceutical Industry

'Our accent is on diabetes. I hope other groups will look at treating other things, such as Parkinson's disease or Alzheimer's. If you have more and more groups involved in stem cell research it can only bring benefit.'

A case for cloning

This vital research can save lives

The news that Newcastle scientists have applied for permission to clone human embryos – as a route to developing new treatments for diabetes – is an inescapable outcome of the House of Lords' recent amendments to the Human Embryology Act. Once these legislative changes were made, it was never a question of 'if' this sort of work would go ahead, but 'when'. This has not stopped anti-abortion groups from reacting to the proposed experiment with outrage and horror. To these organisations, such projects are unethical, are unlikely to achieve the goals promised by medical researchers, and could lead to new biological horrors. Such claims are all open to challenge, however.

For a start, the proposed experiments will not lead to the creation of carbon-copy humans, the slippery-slope argument that is often put forward by opponents. Reproductive cloning is completely banned under the embryo act. Nor is it true that embryos will be created purely to meet researchers' needs. The eggs that will be used as the basis for these experiments will be ones left over from IVF treatments. These would normally be disposed of. Now, researchers – after gaining donors' permission – will use them to create their embryo clones. They will then provide the stem cells that, in turn, could be transformed into pancreatic cells for transplanting into patients. The power of this technique is that it could create tissue that exactly matches individual patients' genetic constituents. No other technique can hope to do this. Thus the claims – that cloning will do nothing new – must be seen as highly suspect.

There is no guarantee the project will lead to perfect transplants. But until this work can be attempted, scientists will always be hampered in their effort to cure degenerative illnesses such as diabetes. The Newcastle project should therefore be welcomed – and approved.

■ This article first appeared in *The Observer*, 13 June 2004.

Scientists get go-ahead to clone first human embryo

By Roger Highfield

British scientists were given a licence yesterday to create Europe's first cloned human embryo for research.

An attempt could be made by the team in Newcastle upon Tyne as early as mid-August 2004, placing the country at the forefront of world-wide efforts to create a revolutionary generation of medical treatments.

Scientists such as Dr Ian Wilmut, who cloned Dolly the sheep, welcomed the news as the first step in an effort to provide new insights into illness and ways to grow a patient's own cells to treat a vast range of diseases, from Alzheimer's to Parkinson's.

But the decision was condemned by pro-life campaigners as tragic and frightening. It marked the manipulation, exploitation and trivialisation of human life, they said.

The Human Fertilisation and Embryology Authority gave the Newcastle team permission to study how to clone early human embryos efficiently and use them as a source of stem cells with the potential to develop into any type for medical treatments and to understand disease.

The authority emphasised: 'Stem cells created under this licence will be used for research only.'

It is the first time such work has been approved in Europe.

Prof Alison Murdoch, one of the team, said she was 'thrilled' and added: 'There is no reason why we can't do it next week.'

When the application was submitted in February by Prof Murdoch, of the Newcastle NHS Fertility Centre, and Dr Miodrag Stojkovic, of Newcastle University, the aim was to develop a treatment for diabetes and to reach the point where a Type 1 diabetic's tissue could be grown for transplant.

But the image of therapeutic cloning as a potential cure-all received a dent when it emerged that the overall aim of the original application was questioned by a committee of the Fertilisation and Embryology Authority.

Because it raised legal issues that could be seized upon by pro-life campaigners, the team at Newcastle's Centre for Life has dropped this aim for the time being.

Dr Denise Faustman, a researcher in diabetes at Harvard Medical School, said a 'paradigm shift' in diabetes research had occurred that placed more emphasis on alternative approaches.

'We have had overwhelming support from senior scientists and clinicians from all over the world and many letters from patients who may benefit from the research'

Pro-life groups, such as Comment on Reproductive Ethics (Core), say that stem cells created from a cloned embryo of a diabetic may suffer the same disorder.

They cite evidence from studies of mice that the stem cells may proliferate out of control and provoke immune reactions.

Core said it was taking legal advice on the legality of the cloning licence. Josephine Quintavalle, a spokesman, also questioned whether there was a conflict of interest in the role of Prof Murdoch as head of the fertility unit that provides eggs for cloning and her role in submitting the application to use the eggs.

Prof Murdoch said: 'We have had overwhelming support from senior scientists and clinicians from all over the world and many letters from patients who may benefit from the research.

'Realistically, we have at least five years of further laboratory work to do before we move to clinical trials but this could be reduced if we receive additional funding.'

Dr Stojkovic said he was surprised and pleased that the licence had been granted.

He said: 'Newcastle is now the national front-runner in this area of research but pressure is mounting in America for its scientists to be allowed to do this work.

'If we are to stay at the cutting edge, we must obtain further financial backing or, as has happened before, Britain will lose out.'

The decision means that the Newcastle team could become only the second in the world to carry out human cloning successfully.

This year scientists in South Korea said they had produced the first human cloned embryos, although some scientists have said the work is not definitive.

Suzi Leather, the chairman of the Human Fertilisation and Embryology Authority, said: 'After careful consideration of all the scientific, ethical, legal and medical aspects of the project, the licence committee agreed to grant an initial one-year research licence to the Newcastle Centre for Life.

'In Britain, research on human embryos is permitted only for certain purposes.

'The purpose of this research is to increase knowledge about the development of embryos and enable this knowledge to be applied in developing treatments for serious disease.

'This research is preliminary. It is not aimed at specific illnesses.'

CHAPTER TWO: ANIMAL CLONING

The world of science fiction

How the world of science fiction became fact in only 10 years

By David Derbyshire Science Correspondent

A decade ago most serious scientists believed that cloning adult mammals was impossible.

How could a single cell removed from an animal's udder or ovary be persuaded to behave like a newly conceived embryo? It was pure science fiction.

A lot can happen in 10 years. Since the announcement of Dolly the sheep in 1997, more than half a dozen species have been cloned.

The cloning era began in 1985 when Steen Willadsen, a Danish researcher, cloned a lamb from a sheep embryo. A cow cloned from embryo cells followed. The animals were cloned using a technique called nuclear transfer: the swapping of a cell nucleus into a hollowed-out unfertilised egg.

Nuclear transfer was relatively easy using embryo cells. What made Dolly special was that she was cloned from an adult sheep, using a sample of tissue removed from the udder of a six-year-old Finn Dorset ewe at the Roslin Institute, near Edinburgh, by Dr Ian Wilmut and Dr Keith Campbell.

Dolly was followed by a cloned mouse, cow, goat, pig and cat. Last year Ralph the rat and a cloned horse called Idoha Gem joined the menagerie.

Despite the successes, cloning remains risky and unpredictable. Dolly was the only success from 277 attempts. Most of her siblings miscarried, while a few were badly deformed.

Dolly was followed by a cloned mouse, cow, goat, pig and cat. Last year Ralph the rat and a cloned horse called Idoha Gem joined the menagerie

Failure rates in other species have been high. Dolly died prematurely last year, raising concerns that clones may age faster than normally conceived animals.

Scientists have also failed to clone monkeys in hundreds of attempts. Some believe there may be particular difficulties in cloning primates, the group that includes humans.

Despite the problems, there has been no shortage of publicity seekers saying that they are keen to try. First off the mark was an American physicist, Dr Richard Seed, who said in 1998 that he was ready to begin.

In January 2001 Severino Antinori, a controversial Italian fertility doctor, announced similar plans. By the end of November 2002 he had claimed that the first baby would be born in January 2003. The baby has yet to be produced.

At Christmas 2002 the American Raelian UFO cult claimed that it had cloned a baby but again failed to come up with proof.

The most recent before the Korean team to make human cloning claims was Dr Panos Zavos, an American fertility scientist. Last month he said he had implanted a cloned embryo in a woman but later said she had failed to become pregnant. His announcement was condemned by mainstream scientists.

Cloning concerns

Information from www.cherrybyte.org

Cloning sheep involves removing the nucleus from an egg cell of a ewe and transferring in a nucleus from another cell in her body.

Cloning of farm animals, pioneered by Professor Ian Wilmut at the Roslin Institute in Scotland, is a technology that could generate important benefits for human health. Sheep, for example, can be genetically engineered to produce therapeutic proteins in their milk that can be used to treat diseases in people. If these sheep can be cloned in sufficient numbers, these treatments could be made widely available for those who need them most. The cloning technology could also be used to make human stem cells from the embryonic ball of cells that is formed before implantation. These stem cells may provide new ways to treat presently incurable diseases such as Parkinson's disease.

There are two major concerns about the future of cloning technology. The first is whether it's ethically acceptable to use animals or human embryos in this way. This is a matter for public debate and government legislation.

The second is that the technology is far from perfect, and this is an area where scientists have work still to do. The birth of Dolly, the first cloned sheep, was the first success in over 270 attempts, many of which produced aborted embryos and developmental defects. Understanding the causes of these failures and preventing them recurring in the future would be a major step towards easing animal welfare concerns and making the technology acceptable to the general public. And now, in February 2001, Dr Lorraine Young and her colleagues at the Roslin Institute and the Scottish Agricultural College have taken a major step forward in reducing developmental abnormalities in cloned animals, by pinpointing the cause of one of the major birth defects.

By Dr Phil Gates

Key steps in cloning

Animal embryos normally develop when a nucleus in the mother's egg cell fuses with a father's sperm nucleus. The nucleus from each parent contains genetic information in sets of chromosomes. In normal sexual reproduction each parent contributes only half the total number of chromosomes needed for the development of an embryo, so the offspring carries characteristics of both parents.

There are two major concerns about the future of cloning technology. The first is whether it's ethically acceptable . . . the second is that the technology is far from perfect

When sheep are cloned the nucleus is removed from a mother's egg cell and is replaced with a nucleus from another cell in her body, or more often with a nucleus from another sheep. This contains a full set of chromosomes with all the genetic information needed to produce an embryo without a contribution from male sperm. The egg cell with its transplanted nucleus is cultured in the laboratory until it begins to form an embryo, then this is implanted in the sheep's womb to complete its development. The cloned lamb only has genes from its mother, so it's a near-perfect genetic copy of her. The process of nuclear transfer does not produce truly identical clones as some genes are not present in the nucleus of the mother's cell but in other structures known as mitochondria. The mitochondria already present in the egg cell also have influence on the cloned individual and not just the genes from the donor nucleus.

Large offspring syndrome

One of the commonest causes of abnormalities in cloned cattle and sheep is a dramatic increase in birth weight, which endangers the mother and her offspring. But recently Dr Lorraine Young has identified the cause of the problem. It's called IGF2R (Insulin Growth Factor 2

Receptor) and is a protein which regulates the growth of embryos. Abnormally large embryos have an unusually low level of IGF2R, compared with normal embryos, so affected cloned embryos overgrow from early in gestation until just before birth, leading to Large Offspring Syndrome.

So why don't cloned embryos produce enough IGF2R? Dr Young's experiments show that the gene that produces the protein doesn't have an essential chemical modification – known as methylation – which controls how much protein the gene will produce. Something in the cloning process disrupts the normal process of methylation.

Exactly what causes this failure is still a mystery, but research so far from the Roslin scientists already represents a major step forward in improving the welfare of cloned sheep. They are now developing a screening technique to identify embryos producing too little IGF2R while they're still in culture, so only embryos with the correct amount of the protein – that will produce lambs with normal birth weight – will be implanted in the mother.

The future

The recent news that scientists in Italy and the United States of America propose to begin cloning humans for childless couples made headlines in the press and has generated a wave of protest worldwide. Some people find it ethically abhorrent to treat humans in this way. Others see benefits for mankind but point to the high failure rate in cloning farm animals, where abnormalities and birth defects are common. There is deep concern about the possibility of accidentally producing large numbers of deformed human foetuses for every successful clone that is born. If cloning of humans ever does go ahead, it will depend on the development of sophisticated screening techniques that detect defective embryos at the earliest stage in cloning – in the laboratory – long before the embryo is implanted in a mother and begins the advanced stages of development.

The research being pioneered at the Roslin Institute, home of the first successful cloned mammal, is aimed fairly and squarely at ensuring the highest standards of welfare during the cloning of farm animals. It will also assist safe development of human stem cells for disease therapy. If society in general decides that use of stem cells from cloned human embryos can be permitted, then the research in progress will lay the foundations for ensuring that it can be done safely.

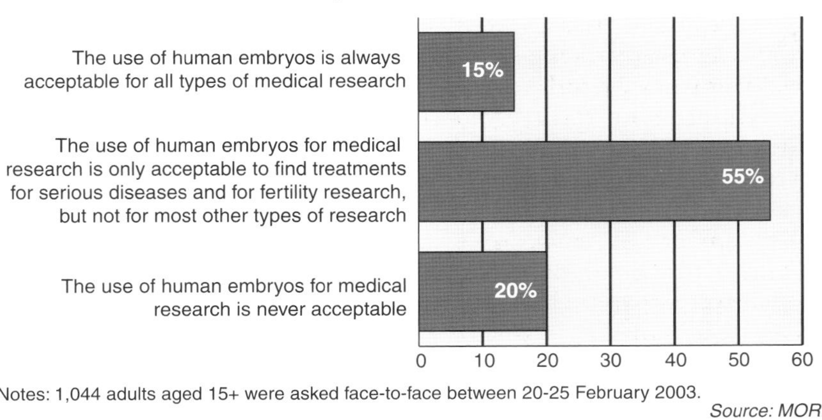

Safer cloning on the way

When Dolly – the first cloned sheep – was born in 1997 she created worldwide headlines for the team of scientists at the Roslin Institute in Scotland whose test-tube techniques produced her. It seemed that flocks of cloned, genetically engineered sheep producing life-saving drugs in their milk might soon be grazing on farms.

But many people were troubled by the welfare implications of cloned farm animals. Dolly was the first success in over 270 attempts, which had failed because the embryos died from defects like Large Offspring Syndrome, where they sometimes grow up to twice the normal size. It seemed to be a hit-and-miss technology, with a heavy price to pay in terms of premature embryo deaths.

Gene screen

Now the latest research from Dr Lorraine Young at the Roslin Institute and her colleagues at the Scottish Agricultural College has taken a major step forward in reducing the risk of birth defects in cloned animals. They've discovered a shortage of a protein in cloned embryos that's vital for switching off their growth, and have found the gene responsible. Dr Young's discovery means that the scientists can now develop a laboratory screening technique during the earliest stages of embryo development that will identify defective embryos and ensure that only normal ones are implanted in their surrogate mothers.

The research at the Roslin Institute is an important step along the road towards safer, more humane cloning of farm animals

■ The above information is from www.cherrybyte.org

Should we clone animals?

Despite all the fuss about human cloning it may never happen. Animal cloning is already done in many species, and raises some important ethical issues which we look at here

What's the church doing here?

Since 1993, the Church of Scotland's Society, Religion and Technology Project (SRT) has examined the ethics of genetic engineering and cloning in animals and plants with an expert working group. This work produced the book *Engineering Genesis*, now a standard text on the ethics of GM issues. The group included Professor Ian Wilmut, leader of the Roslin Institute team that created Dolly the cloned sheep. So when Dolly hit the headlines in February 1997, the church was already in a position to offer a balanced and informed view on cloning issues. That May the Church of Scotland General Assembly was one of the first organisations in the world to give a considered official view on animal and human cloning. SRT continues to be engaged in national and international ethical discussions about cloning issues, and has written and broadcast widely. To help shed light on these confused and often misrepresented issues, we've produced 3 information sheets – one on animal cloning, one on human cloning and one on human embryonic stem cells.

Is cloning animals simply wrong?

Cloning occurs naturally in many plants and micro-organisms, and some lower animals, but it does not normally happen in humans and mammals, except for identical twins. Should we respect this biological distinction or celebrate our capacity to override it? It's not a new issue. The first cloned sheep were created in 1979. For creatures that rely on sexual reproduction it is important for a healthy population to maintain good genetic diversity. Cloning such creatures could therefore be seen as a step in the wrong direction. For Christians and many others the very God-given diversity and variety in nature is a cause of praise to its creator, vital for the species, and of pleasure and use to humans. Where God evolves a system of boundless possibilities by diversification, ought humans to select certain functions we think are the best, and simply replicate them? Does cloning animals exceed other ethical limits? In our other cloning sheet we argue why human cloning is ethically unacceptable. One reason is its instrumental effect of predetermining people's genetics. This would not itself be an absolute objection to cloning animals, if we already accept a certain amount of valid human use of animals. As we shall see there are problems of animal harm, but there are also intrinsic issues. As with genetic modification, cloning is a serious intervention which some feel violates the value inherent in the animal. We think a 'No, unless . . .' approach should be taken. Animal cloning should not be done without a very good reason. Let's look at some possible cases.

Cloning to help make pharmaceuticals in the milk of GM farm animals

The original reason why the Roslin Institute and PPL Therapeutics produced cloned sheep arose from their earlier work to genetically engineer sheep to produce proteins of medical value in their milk. This was one of the least controversial GM applications for the SRT working group and the church. It had clear human benefits and few animal welfare or other concerns, once past the experimental stage. But the modification process was imprecise, long and expensive, and used many animals. Nuclear transfer cloning provided a technical solution which enabled scientists to produce GM 'founder' animals directly from modified cells with greater certainty and precision, which would then be bred normally. It was used to produce Polly, the first sheep to be both cloned and genetically modified, and various other lines of GM sheep. The Church of Scotland accepted animal

cloning in this limited context, aimed at using less animals to address a clear medical need, where cloning was not the main intention, and where natural methods would not work. Since then, however, it has been largely abandoned because many welfare problems arose in the cloned sheep.

Dolly, cloning and animal welfare

Dolly was a sensational sideline to this research. Her creation rewrote the laws of biology because she showed that ordinary (somatic) body cells could be turned back to embryos and made into new offspring, genetically identical to the animal whose cells had been used. Cloning has now been done experimentally, usually with much unjustified hype, in cattle, pigs, goats, mice, rabbits, one cat, horses and even infertile mules, but not so far in dogs, primates or humans. Efficiency is usually very low and with the notable exception of pigs, serious animal welfare problems have generally occurred. These include perinatal and birth problems, oversized offspring and disease susceptibility, but it's not clear if premature ageing occurs. Some scientists think that somatic cell cloning has an inherent problem of incomplete reprogramming of the DNA in the cell nucleus. The UK Farm Animal Welfare Council was clearly right to call for a moratorium on nuclear transfer cloning in commercial agriculture until much more is understood of the causes of these problems.

Animal cloning for novel uses?

Many other uses have been suggested for animal cloning. Cloning gives scientists a tool to do targeted genetic modification. One application has been to try and eliminate genes that lead to the rejection of pig organs that might be used for future transplants to humans. Xenotransplantation is ethically controversial. Cloning pigs for this purpose is only justified if the result would make a substantial improvement to patient survival and quality of life, and if pig virus transmission risks were overcome. Currently this seems doubtful. Cloning pets is misconceived. One would never recreate a loved companion animal, and may make many suffering animals in the process. Even if millionaires provide the money it is a trivialisation of scientific skills. Cloned prime sporting animals like horses or camels seem unjustified because so many other factors could overrule the performance. Conservationists are sceptical of the value of cloning to save rare animals. It would be impractical to create enough numbers to make the difference between survival and extinction, but in less threatened species it might be useful to preserve rare genetic stock for the future.

Cloning in farm animal production

The main applied use of cloning so far has been in farm animal production. Most dairy cattle in the UK are already produced by artificial insemination. Semen from one select bull services numerous cows. Embryo transfer goes a step further. Why not clone prime cattle in a breeding programme, to raise more breeding stock to the highest level of 'genetic merit', or even clone the best beasts for fattening for slaughter? The Church of Scotland takes the view that to clone animals routinely for production is treating animals too instrumentally, given that natural methods of breeding exist. A case might be made if cloning helped spread a genetic modification to combat an animal disease like foot and mouth, but mere commercial production or supermarket efficiency are not enough to justify cloning. Copying the complete genetic blueprint for efficiency's sake carries a factory mass production mentality too far into animal husbandry. Our fellow creatures are more than identical widgets on an assembly line. There are limits on how far we should commodify animals for their functional worth. We may use them, but we also need to remind ourselves that they are God's creatures first, to whom we may not do everything we like. Given the abuses which a commercial drive has led to in some areas of animal production, cloning is normally a place to draw a line.

Cloning has now been done experimentally, usually with much unjustified hype, in cattle, pigs, goats, mice, horses, but not so far in dogs, primates or humans

■ For our book *Engineering Genesis* or more about these or other ethical issues in technology, contact the Society, Religion and Technology Project. See page 41 for our address details.

Animal cloning

Information from the Dr Hadwen Trust for Humane Research

Cloning and genetic modification of animals is the only area of animal experimentation that has substantially increased in recent years, whilst all other types of animal experiments are in decline. Animal species that have been cloned so far include mouse, rat, rabbit, sheep, cat, horse, mule, pig, and cow.

The process of cloning animals inflicts considerable suffering and distress, and breaches the intrinsic value of individual animals. Animal cloning is being conducted out of curiosity or is profit driven. Animals have been cloned as convenient 'production units' for meat, as a source of organs, and as 'bioreactors' to produce proteins in their milk or urine. Inflicting suffering on sentient creatures in this way in the pursuit of profits is ethically unacceptable.

The Italian and American scientists who cloned a horse and mule respectively intend their work to assist in the production of valuable racehorses.[1, 2] The private financier who bankrolled the cloning of a kitten in Texas, intends to charge pet owners for cloning their animals.[3] In Australia 90% of cloned lambs die soon after birth due to abnormalities, in research aimed at improving profits for the wool industry.[4]

Claims that cloned animals will be of enormous benefit to medical science are highly speculative and far from proven. The company PPL Therapeutics is cloning genetically engineered pigs as a source of organs for transplants. The feasibility of such cross-species transplants (so-called xenotransplants) ever being successfully conducted in humans is increasingly doubtful and fraught with risk. Furthermore, an opt-out system of organ donation, instead of an opt-in system with donor cards as in the UK, together with investment in the transplant services, has effectively ended the

shortfall of organs in Spain – yet such a simple solution has no commercial potential.

Cloning is extremely inefficient and wasteful of animal lives. Hundreds of cloned embryos have to be created to produce just one or two live offspring. Dolly the sheep for example was the only survivor out of 277 cloned embryos. Cloned embryos implanted into surrogate mothers can often miscarry, causing pain and distress. It is not unusual for cloned animals to die from infections shortly after birth or to be born with deformities such as underdeveloped lungs, bloodstream imbalances, abnormalities of the kidney, liver and brain, enlarged tongues, intestinal blockages, diabetes, immune system deficiencies and shortened tendons.[5]

Cloning is extremely inefficient and wasteful of animal lives. Hundreds of cloned embryos have to be created to produce just one or two live offspring

Surviving clones have developed unpredictable health problems. For example, three cloned piglets that had appeared completely healthy recently died from sudden and unexpected heart attacks at only 6 months old.[6] Dolly the sheep suffered from arthritis at an early age and was put down because of an incurable lung disease. Scientists are now questioning whether any cloned animal can ever be entirely normal, a consideration which has major implications for their future usefulness in medical research.

Reference

1 *Nature* 2003, 7 August, Vol 424, p 635
2 *The Guardian*, 30 May 2003
3 *The Telegraph*, 15 February 2002
4 *Sydney Morning Herald*, Australia, 28 November 2001
5 *New Scientist* 2001, 19 May pp 14-15
6 *New Scientist* 2003, 6 September p12

■ The Dr Hadwen Trust for Humane Research is a registered medical research charity. The Trust is founded on anti-vivisection principles and is opposed to all animal experiments, for both ethical and scientific reasons. The trust aims to encourage, fund and promote the development and use of non-animal methods to replace animals in medical research. For more information please visit their website at www.drhadwentrust.org.uk or contact them via e-mail at info@drhadwentrust.org.uk.

Animal cloning

Information from the Research Defence Society (RDS)

Dolly the sheep may have been the world's most famous clone, but she was not the first. Cloning creates a genetically identical copy of an animal or plant. Many animals – including frogs, mice, sheep, and cows – had been cloned before Dolly. Plants are often cloned – when you take a cutting, you are producing a clone. Human identical twins are also clones.

So Dolly was not the first clone, and she looked like any other sheep, so why did she cause so much excitement and concern? Because she was the first mammal to be cloned from an adult cell, rather than an embryo. This was a major scientific achievement, but also raised ethical concerns.

Since 1996, when Dolly was born, other sheep have been cloned from adult cells, as have mice, rabbits, horses and donkeys, pigs, goats and cattle. In 2004 a mouse was cloned using a nucleus from an olfactory neuron, showing that the donor nucleus can come from a tissue of the body that does not normally divide.

How was Dolly produced?

Producing an animal clone from an adult cell is obviously much more complex and difficult than growing a plant from a cutting. So when scientists working at the Roslin Institute in Scotland produced Dolly, the only lamb born from 277 attempts, it was a major news story around the world.

To produce Dolly, the scientists used the nucleus of an udder cell from a six-year-old Finn Dorset white sheep. The nucleus contains nearly all the cell's genes. They had to find a way to 'reprogramme' the udder cells – to keep them alive but stop them growing – which they achieved by altering the growth medium (the 'soup' in which the cells were kept alive). Then they injected the cell into an unfertilised egg cell which had had its nucleus removed, and made the cells fuse by using electrical

pulses. The unfertilised egg cell came from a Scottish Blackface ewe.

When the scientists had managed to fuse the nucleus from the adult white sheep cell with the egg cell from the black-faced sheep, they needed to make sure that the resulting cell would develop into an embryo. They cultured it for six or seven days to see if it divided and developed normally, before implanting it into a surrogate mother, another Scottish Blackface ewe. Dolly had a white face.

From 277 cell fusions, 29 early embryos developed and were implanted into 13 surrogate mothers. But only one pregnancy went to full term, and the 6.6kg Finn Dorset lamb 6LLS (alias Dolly) was born after 148 days.

Why are scientists interested in cloning?

The main reason that the scientists at Roslin wanted to be able to clone sheep and other large animals was connected with their research aimed at producing medicines in the milk of such animals. Researchers have managed to transfer human genes that produce useful proteins into sheep and cows, so that they can produce, for instance, the blood clotting agent factor IX to treat haemophilia or alpha-1-antitrypsin to treat cystic fibrosis and other lung conditions.

Cloned animals could also be developed that would produce human antibodies against infectious diseases and even cancers. 'Foreign' genes have been transplanted into zebra fish, which are widely used in laboratories, and embryos cloned from these fish express the foreign protein. If this technique can be applied to mammalian cells and the cells cultured to produce cloned animals, these could then breed conventionally to form flocks of genetically engineered animals all producing medicines in their milk.

There are other medical and scientific reasons for the interest in cloning. It is already being used alongside genetic techniques in the development of animal organs for transplant into humans (xenotransplantation). Combining such genetic techniques with cloning of pigs (achieved for the first time in March 2000) would lead to a reliable supply of suitable donor organs. The use of pig organs has been hampered by the presence of a sugar, alpha gal, on pig cells, but in 2002 scientists succeeded in knocking out the gene that makes it, and these 'knockout' pigs could be bred naturally. How-

ever, there are still worries about virus transmission.

The study of animal clones and cloned cells could lead to greater understanding of the development of the embryo and of ageing and age-related diseases. Cloned mice become obese, with related symptoms such as raised plasma insulin and leptin levels, though their offspring do not and are normal. Cloning could be used to create better animal models of diseases, which could in turn lead to further progress in understanding and treating those diseases. It could even enhance biodiversity by ensuring the continuation of rare breeds and endangered species.

What happened to Dolly?

Dolly, probably the most famous sheep in the world, lived a pampered existence at the Roslin Institute. She mated and produced normal offspring in the normal way, showing that such cloned animals can reproduce. Born on 5 July 1996, she was euthanased on 14 February 2003, aged six and a half. Sheep can live to age 11 or 12, but Dolly suffered from arthritis in a hind leg joint and from sheep pulmonary adenomatosis, a virus-induced lung tumour to which sheep raised indoors are prone. On 2 February 2003, Australia's first cloned sheep died unexpectedly at the age of two years and 10 months. The cause of death was unknown and the carcass was quickly cremated as it was decomposing.

Dolly's chromosomes were a little shorter than those of other sheep, but in most other ways she was the same as any other sheep of her chronological age. However, her early ageing may reflect that she was raised from the nucleus of a 6-year-old sheep. Study of her cells also revealed that the very small amount of DNA outside the nucleus, in the mitochondria of the cells, is all inherited from the donor egg cell, not from the donor nucleus like the rest of her DNA. So she is not a completely identical copy. This finding could be important for sex-linked diseases such as haemophilia, and certain neuromuscular, brain and kidney conditions that are passed on through the mother's side of the family only.

Improving the technology

Scientists are working on ways to improve the technology. For example, when two genetically identical cloned mice embryos are combined, the aggregate embryo is more likely to survive to birth. Improvements in the culture medium may also help.

Ethical concerns and regulation

Most of the ethical concerns about cloning relate to the possibility that it might be used to clone humans. There would be enormous technical difficulties. As the technology stands at present, it would have to involve women willing to donate perhaps hundreds of eggs, surrogate pregnancies with high rates of miscarriage and stillbirth, and the possibility of premature ageing and high cancer rates for any children so produced. However, in 2004 South Korean scientists announced that they had cloned 30 human embryos, grown them in the laboratory until they were a hollow ball of cells, and produced a line of stem cells from them. Further news is awaited.

In the USA, President Clinton asked the National Bioethics Commission and Congress to examine the issues, and in the UK the House of Commons Science and Technology Committee, the Human Embryology and Fertilisation Authority and the Human Genetics Advisory Commission all consulted widely and advised that human cloning should be banned. The Council of Europe has banned human cloning: in fact most countries have banned the use of cloning to produce human babies (human reproductive cloning). However, there is one important medical aspect of cloning technology that could be applied to humans, which people may find less objectionable. This is therapeutic cloning (or cell nucleus replacement) for tissue engineering, in which tissues, rather than a baby, are created.

In therapeutic cloning, single cells would be taken from a person and 'reprogrammed' to create stem cells, which have the potential to develop into any type of cell in the body. When needed, the stem cells could be thawed and then induced to grow into particular types of cell such as heart, liver or brain cells that could be used in medical treatment. Reprogramming cells is likely to prove technically difficult.

Therapeutic cloning research is already being conducted in animals, and stem cells have been grown by this method and transplanted back into the original donor animal. In humans, this technique would revolutionise cell and tissue transplantation as a method of treating diseases. However, it is a very new science and has raised ethical concerns. In the UK a group headed by the Chief Medical Officer, Professor Liam Donaldson, has recommended that research on early human embryos should be allowed. The Human Fertilisation and Embryology Act was amended in 2001 to allow the use of embryos for stem cell research and consequently the HFEA has the responsibility for regulating all embryonic stem cell research in the UK. There is a potential supply of early embryos as patients undergoing in-vitro fertilisation usually produce a surplus of fertilised eggs.

As far as animal cloning is concerned, all cloning for research or medical purposes in the UK must be approved by the Home Office under the strict controls of the Animals (Scientific Procedures) Act 1986. This safeguards animal welfare while allowing important scientific and medical research to go ahead.

■ The above information is from the Research Defence Society's website which can be found at www.rds-online.org.uk

Endangered species gain a place on Frozen Ark

By Helen Johnstone

Scientists are developing the world's first DNA and tissue bank to preserve thousands of animals facing extinction, in an international project called the Frozen Ark.

Hundreds of species become extinct every week and thousands more are expected to disappear over the next 30 years.

They include 1,130 species (24 per cent) of mammals and 1,183 species (12 per cent) of birds, according to a report presented to the United Nations Environmental Programme. Under the initiative, launched 26 July 2004, tissue from thousands of mammals, birds, insects and reptiles will be frozen to ensure that genetic blueprints are secured, to be used if the species die out.

Priority is to be given to animals in danger within the next five years and those already extinct in the wild. The first entrants to the Frozen Ark will include the yellow seahorse, a small fish depleted partly by trade in traditional Chinese medicine.

Another is the British field cricket, whose population by the early 1990s was reduced to a single colony of fewer than 100 in West Sussex. Polynesian tree snails, first recorded on volcanic islands of the Pacific during Cook's voyage of 1774, will also be included. The introduction of a predatory snail wiped out half of the original 100 species.

Without the Frozen Ark – an initiative between the Natural History Museum, the Zoological Society of London and the Institute of Genetics at Nottingham University – researchers say the world would be left with only brief descriptions in scientific papers and specimens in museums.

It will build a global list of DNA collections and future biologists could find many more uses once its world-wide network of complementary banks is up and running.

'We are cautious about cloning because it gets so sexed up, but who knows what we will be using these specimens for in the future?'

Prof Phil Rainbow, the keeper of zoology at the National History Museum, said: 'Natural catastrophes apart, the current rate of animal loss is the greatest in the history of the Earth and the fate of species is desperate. For future biologists and conservationists and for the animals they seek to protect this network will be of immeasurable value.'

Scientists also admit the samples could be used to create clones of extinct animals.

Prof Alan Cooper, the director of the Henry Wellcome Ancient Biomolecules Centre at Oxford University and a member of the Frozen Ark steering committee, said: 'I think it will be used for cloning eventually.

'We are cautious about cloning because it gets so sexed up, but who knows what we will be using these specimens for in the future?'

Dr Anne McClaren, who chairs the committee, said the primary motive was an ethical one. 'I think Noah would have been proud of this project.'

Cloning

Information from Europeans For Medical Advancement

Sensational claims from bizarre religious sects notwithstanding, nobody has yet cloned a human baby. But in February 2004, scientists in South Korea successfully cloned human embryos to the blastocyst (ball of cells) stage for the first time. Why? Not in an attempt to create a living child but to create stem cells for transplantation into patients with diseases such as Parkinson's, diabetes and osteoarthritis. These are diseases where tissue has failed or been destroyed and could be replaced with new tissue created by 'therapeutic cloning' – something very different from cloning a new person.

Even therapeutic cloning is controversial because many people believe it is unethical to destroy human embryos. But the idea of cloning people is almost universally regarded as ethically abhorrent. One argument frequently advanced against human cloning is the fact that cloning animals has been so fraught with difficulties and failures.

Despite the fact that several species of animals have now been cloned, scientists still encounter new obstacles with every new species. Dolly the sheep was the world's most famous cloned animal. She suffered premature arthritis and died unnaturally early, but most other cloned animals have not fared nearly so well. Cloned animals of every species have suffered from a catalogue of deformities, such as malformed hearts, lungs, intestines, immune systems and many other ills. Only around 5% of cloned embryos survive until birth and of the few that are born live, most have a lethal defect and die within days or weeks. Dolly was the only survivor of 277 embryos. Many of the surrogate mothers also die during the pregnancies.

But these experiences in animals have very little relevance for humans. Some researchers believe the gross abnormalities suffered by cloned animals would be less likely to occur in humans – but there is no way of

knowing without actually trying it out.

This is always the case with animal experiments. What happens in animals is no guide to what will happen in humans. Infect chimpanzees with HIV, for example, and they will not contract AIDS. The first people to try a new procedure or medicine are the real guinea pigs. In France in the 1980s, thousands of people were given HIV-contaminated blood transfusions because chimpanzees had indicated it was safe.

Reproductive cloning of animals is of no medical value for people. But it does illustrate some important biological principles. It shows that knowledge gained from one species does not usually translate to another. (Knowing how to clone sheep does not make it easier to clone cows.) And it shows how wrong our original ideas were about clones being identical copies of their 'parents'. Cc, the world's first cloned cat, was a different colour from the much-loved pet she was supposed to replace – clearly illustrating that even though two individuals may have exactly the same genes, they can still be quite different, because gene expression is affected by environmental and other factors too. In fact, most mammals have pretty much the same genes as each other – it is differences in expression that make each species unique. This is why extrapolating results from animal experiments to humans – or even from rats to mice – fails more often than not but in a completely unpredictable way: because gene expression is complex. Linear extrapolation does not work and this is the reason why.

Therapeutic cloning of human cells, on the other hand, is potentially of great medical value and if adult, rather than embryonic cells can be used this should be a medical advance to please everybody.

Scientific advisers: Dr Ray Greek, Dr Jean Greek, Professor Niall Shanks, Professor Lawrence Hansen, Dr Nancy Harrison, Dr Christopher Anderegg, Dr Claude Reiss

■ The above information is from Europeans For Medical Advancement. For further information visit their website: www.curedisease.com

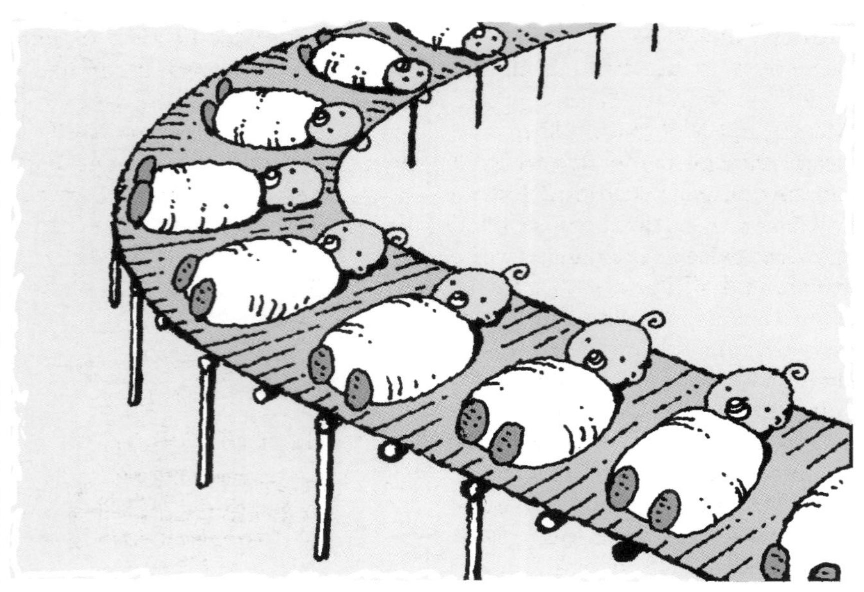

Genetics

A bit of this and a bit of that

Cloning

What is cloning?

Cloning means the production of genetically identical animals. In 1995 scientists at the Roslin Institute in Edinburgh, Scotland, produced Megan and Morag – two lambs cloned from a single embryo. Two years later, Dolly was produced, the first example of a clone produced not from an embryo cell but from a cell taken from an adult sheep. She was cloned using a nuclear transfer technique, where the nucleus from a cell taken from the mammary gland of an adult sheep was fused with an unfertilised egg from which the nucleus had been removed. 277 cells were fused in this way, resulting in 29 viable embryos which were implanted into surrogate Blackface ewes. One gave birth to Dolly.

Animal welfare

Cloning involves many possibilities for detrimental effects on animals. For example, cloned lambs and calves are frequently abnormally large at birth – some have been twice normal size. One cloning expert admitted in 1992 that 'many cloned calves are abnormal'.[1] In Australia, a lamb of five times the mean birth weight for the breed has been recorded. In addition, cloned animals are often found to have malformed internal organs.[2] Both of these adverse effects were seen in the first Edinburgh experiments in 1995 that led to Megan and Morag. In addition to death through malformed internal organs, one lamb had to be delivered by Caesarean section because it had grown to twice its normal size in the womb, and all but one of the five cloned lambs were at least 20% larger than they should have been. Immediately after birth many cloned lambs have breathing difficulties, are lethargic and often will not suckle. As a consequence, perinatal mortality is high. Miscarriage rates are also high; this is thought to be at least in part because of 'large offspring syndrome'.[3]

Cloning techniques also require a great deal of surgical intervention. Those sheep destined to be egg donors undergo hormone injections, followed by surgery to have the egg cells removed. Following nuclear transfer, it is common for the cloned embryos to be surgically implanted into temporary recipient sheep. Six days later, these temporary 'foster mothers' are simply killed and the embryos removed. The embryos are then placed, again surgically, into the surrogate mother ewes. Some deliveries have been achieved via Caesarean section. So the process is far from simple, and the surgery required can reasonably be expected to inflict residual pain.

Attempts to create clones of animals that have been already cloned could also result in increased suffering. In France 1999, a calf which was a clone of a clone died aged eight weeks of rapid depletion of blood cells and severe anaemia. The researchers concluded '. . . somatic cloning may be the cause of long-term deleterious effects'.[4]

One possible application of cloning, suggested by the Roslin team, is the facilitation of farm animal genetic engineering. If successful, the cloning technique could be used to 'mass produce' farm animals which had been genetically engineered to grow faster, bigger or leaner. Cloning could also be used to mass produce animals genetically engineered to produce pharmaceutical proteins in their milk or blood (gene pharming), or for use in xenotransplantation. However, genetic engineering itself has a very poor track record in terms of animal welfare, and the BUAV is appalled at the idea of combining genetic engineering and cloning techniques.

Former Archbishop John Habgood has written of the motives behind cloning experiments:

'But should science be going down this road at all? What is the point of it? The simple answer is – money. The driving force behind most of the research in this field has come from the agricultural industry. I use the word industry deliberately. Cloning is a means of standardising products, and that is what industry always wants.'[5]

It is clear that cloning may cause a great deal of animal suffering. The so-called 'benefits', such as the production of genetically identical herds or flocks of animals for intensive farming, may be seen as dubious or even highly unethical. The BUAV therefore believes that the practice of cloning should be stopped immediately.

Notes on text

1 Seidel, G.E.Jr. Overview of cloning animals by nuclear transplantation. *Proceedings of the Symposium on cloning mammals by nuclear transplantation*, 1992, Colorado State University.
2 Miller, A. Have we, with sheep, gone astray. *The Tablet*, 16 March 1996.
3 *Roslin Institute Annual Report* 1997/98 pp63-64.
4 *The Lancet*, 1 May 1999, Vol. 353, pp1489-91.
5 John Habgood, Send out the clones. *The Observer*, 2 March 1997

■ The above information is from BUAV's website which can be found at www.buav.org

Mouse with two mothers and no father

Mouse with two mothers and no father marks a first for mammals

By Roger Highfield, Science Editor

A mouse has been born that has two mothers, but no father. The animal, named Kaguya – which could prove as controversial as Dolly the cloned sheep – shows for the first time that a particular kind of 'virgin birth' is possible in mammals – and thus people.

The method, perfected by a team at the Tokyo University of Agriculture, with colleagues in Japan and Korea, marks the second advance, after cloning, that appears to make males redundant.

'This is very exciting and impressive,' said Prof Ian Wilmut, head of the team that cloned Dolly.

Although the birth is an amazing feat – so much so that science does not yet have an accepted name for the technique – Prof Wilmut and other scientists stressed that the practical implications were obscure, since the method was even more complex, inefficient and unsafe than cloning.

Sexless reproduction abounds in nature, but not in mammals. Although unfertilised mouse eggs can be jolted into dividing with chemicals or electric shocks, the resulting embryos do not reach term.

In the journal *Nature*, 22 April 2004, Dr Tomohiro Kono and colleagues describe how they produced live female mice, the first being Kaguya, without any need for sperm and male chromosomes.

The animal shows for the first time that a particular kind of 'virgin birth' is possible in mammals – and thus people

Parthenogenesis – reproduction without fertilisation – was thought impossible in mammals due to imprinting, a mechanism that turns genes on and off depending on whether they come from the mother or father. At least 40 genes necessary for development are thought to be regulated in this way.

Rather than combine egg and sperm, Dr Kono combined a female imprinted genetic code from an older egg with a 'male-like' imprinted female genetic code. The latter was created from the genome of a young egg, free of maternal imprinting. To masculinise it, Dr Kono used genetic engineering to remove a gene (H19) so that there was no H19 activity – as is normally the case in the father's genetic code.

Dr Kono told *The Telegraph* that it may be difficult to do this experiment in other species but it 'is a possibility' in some domestic animals. He would not be drawn on whether two women could have a baby this way.

'This is an incredible achievement,' said Prof Azim Surani of the University of Cambridge. But he added that it was too complex to be used on people.

Dr Anne Ferguson-Smith of Cambridge University said: 'This paper does not mean that males are obsolete – the requirement for paternal chromosomes for normal development is still with us.'

You only live twice

By Louisa Pearson

It has no doubt been conducted clandestinely in an underground bunker for years, but the spectre of human cloning in the UK came a step closer in April 2004.

Professor Ian Wilmut, creator of our dearly departed Dolly the sheep, confirmed that Edinburgh's Roslin Institute plans to apply for a licence for 'therapeutic cloning'. Not the mass production of a relaxing spa treatment, but the cloning of human embryos for stem cell research – the body's master cells which can develop into any kind of tissue.

The jury is out on whether the Human Fertilisation and Embryology Authority will grant Wilmut his wish, so we will have to wait a while before we can get Grandma Mark II settled by the fireside.

In the meantime, if you have $50,000 to spare – that is, £28,000 – an American company is offering to clone your pets. The process takes six months and there is one small snag – your clone might be a different colour to the original kitty.

Despite this apparently fundamental flaw in the production of the new Tiddles, Genetic Savings & Clone (GSC) say that five clients have already signed on the dotted line to have their old cats live again.

The Californian company commences cloning next month and the resulting kittens should be ready to take home by November.

Although GSC gives 'a special welcome' to members of the Press on its website, time constraints mean that our communication takes place via e-mail. Its policy of admitting journalists only to its headquarters, and not to its labs, might add fuel to the fire of a suspicious mind.

Mind you, the company does have some impressive credentials. In 1997, Dolly the sheep inspired Arizona millionaire Dr John Sperling to investigate the possibility of cloning his pet dog, Missy. This led to the creation of GSC, which in 2001 funded 'Operation CopyCat' and so brought us CC, the world's first cat clone.

Unfortunately, CC's coat was somewhat different in its colouring from her genetic donor – and GSC warns that this is to be expected of all tortoiseshell cats. So are the cloning company whipping off the white coats and nipping down the cat compound to find a close match? GSC says not. The official explanation is due to something called 'X-linked inactivation' during embryo development. This means that although the clone will bear a close physical resemblance to its genetic donor, it will not be a perfect physical match. If you are still sceptical, GSC points out that DNA evidence was presented to confirm that CC was a true clone.

As animal behaviour is determined by environment as well as genetics, is it really worth paying $50,000 for what is, in effect, a new animal?

Despite this, GSC has been successful in launching a DNA bank for pets. Company spokesman Ben Carlson says that the bank has 'several hundred' clients, including a few from the UK – though, reassuringly, none from Scotland.

To open an account costs $845 initially, then $150 per year, but you get that back, if you go ahead with the full cost of cloning.

But as animal behaviour is determined by environment as well as genetics, is it really worth paying $50,000 for what is, in effect, a new animal?

For GSC's customers, the answer is yes. GSC forwarded *The Scotsman* an e-mail which it claims is from Mary Ann Daniel of Costa Mesa, California, who describes her cat Smokey as 'one in a million', adding that having had him neutered at a young age, cloning is the 'perfect thing'.

Her reference goes on: 'We want to have a cat that has some of his characteristics. Not necessarily all of them, but something.'

Bizarre as this may sound, GSC is not the only US company offering to clone our four-legged friends. The appropriately named PerPETuate and Lazaron are in the market too, thanks to the fact that no US legislation exists to prevent this sort of activity going on. So could it happen over here? In short, no. A report by the government's Animal Procedures Committee in 2001, stated that 'no licences should be issued for trivial objectives, such as the creation or duplication of favourite pets'.

A Home Office spokesman said that no application has ever been submitted for such a licence and that if one does materialise, it will be refused.

But who would want to do such a thing anyway? Why not mourn and move on?

Scottish psychologist Agnes Steven says the British mind-set that pets are part of the family makes the prospect of bringing them back to life irresistible to many. 'Some people don't cope with change and by doing this they're trying to take away the pain of losing a pet.'

Back in Roslin, Wilmut points out that his plan is aimed at developing therapies to help humans with conditions such as motor neurone disease and he says it would be 'immoral' not to forge ahead in this field.

And ethics aside, human cloning might have its up-side, depending on who you clone.

Who could object to a world full of George Clooneys or Julia Roberts? A Hollywood star for every home? We all have our price.

Pet cloning

Ethical FAQ

Are you concerned about the ethics of what you're doing?
We're comfortable with our work, but only because we've made and continue to make careful choices about what we do and how we do it. Before we began our research, we developed a Code of Bioethics, which is unique so far in the biotech industry and which established clear ethical guidelines, especially regarding the treatment of live animals and future uses of our technology. This Code of Bioethics is not merely PR or window dressing; our staff and scientists are contractually bound to follow it.

Given that people who clone their pets might otherwise adopt unwanted pets, aren't you adding to the problem of unwanted dogs and cats?
It may seem counterintuitive, but by doing business with us, our clients are actually *reducing* pet overpopulation. The cloning of any species requires large numbers of eggs for embryo production. In the case of pet species, we purchase these eggs (in the form of whole ovaries) from spay clinics, which would otherwise simply discard them as waste. The clinics then use the cash we provide to spay more dogs and cats, hundreds for every clone we produce. The result is a net reduction in pet overpopulation.

Is GSC exploiting grieving pet owners who have lost their beloved animals and think that cloning will bring them back?
Although we're sensitive to the grief felt by people whose pets have died, most of our clients seek our services while their pets are still alive. Regardless, we help all prospective clients make informed choices based on realistic expectations about cloning. We decline business from people who want us to bring specific pets back to life. Nobody can do that. Our goal is to produce new pets possessing the same genes as previous pets. That's what our clients want and it's a service we can realistically perform.

Isn't this playing God?
Humankind has been shaping nature for thousands of years, since the beginning of agriculture and animal husbandry. We see cloning as a new form of assisted reproduction, not that different from artificial insemination or in vitro fertilisation, perceived by some as 'ungodly' when introduced just decades ago. Ultimately, we consider a strong, tangible Code of Bioethics more meaningful and useful than abstract concerns about 'playing God'.

Isn't cloning cheating death?
We don't see how. Both the genetic donor and the clone, like all living things, will eventually die.

Are you involved in human cloning?
Absolutely not. Our Code of Bioethics forbids any involvement in human cloning and the technology we're developing is unlikely to be useful for human cloning. Dog cloning in particular has numerous species-specific barriers, which is what most of our research is focused on. Human cloning doesn't appear to face such barriers, and thus, the technology we're developing is not needed for human cloning. Furthermore, cloning-related anomalies seen primarily in cattle strongly suggest that human cloning would not be safe for mother or child. To make the technology safe for pet clones and their surrogate mothers, we're investing millions into more advanced cloning methods coupled with advanced embryo assessment by gene array. We see it as ironic, and highly problematic, that no such investment in safeguards is occurring in the human cloning field.

What impact will cloning have on genetic diversity?
Our typical client wishes to obtain a single clone of a mixed breed pet that is spayed, neutered, or beyond breeding age. The clone, therefore, will actually preserve the diversity of the gene pool by preventing the loss of the individual genome. However, the pet population is already so large and varied that concerns over diversity are irrelevant. For endangered species, the big surprise is that cloning may actually increase genetic diversity. There are various reasons why some individuals within an endangered population do not breed, including age, environmental

factors, or simply being at the wrong level for breeding status in that species' social hierarchy. By cloning non-breeding or deceased members of an endangered population, we can potentially increase the genetic diversity of that species. Our policy is that cloning should be the method of last resort for species preservation, because it is far less efficient than habitat preservation, poaching control, and captive breeding. However, for a severely bottlenecked population, cloning may be the only alternative to extinction.

Doesn't pet cloning research result in a lot of dead animals?

Animal cloning research entails the production of large numbers of

cloned embryos, most of which do not survive. The vast majority of such embryos only develop to a few cells in size then fail to implant in the uterus of the surrogate mother. These early embryos have no consciousness. It's misleading to refer to them as 'dead animals'.

Twenty-five per cent of all animals born through cloning using current technology have suffered some kind of cloning-related health problem, ranging from mild to terminal. Fortunately, this has not yet been the case in pet cloning research. We're investing millions in developing embryo assessment technology to ensure that each cloned embryo we transfer to a surrogate mother is normal, and will develop into a healthy cloned pet.

■ The above information is from Genetic Savings & Clone's website which can be found at www.savingsandclone.com

Cloned food

By David Adam

How can we be sure that cloned animals are safe to eat?

We can't be absolutely sure, but the key conclusion scientists reached in November 2003 was that cloned sheep, pigs and cows should be as safe to eat as their non-clone counterparts. And in our post BSE, intensively farmed world, take that whichever way you like.

The suitability for the barbecue or bacon butties of animals created in a laboratory as identical copies of their parent is still largely an academic discussion, because no cloned animal is thought to have entered the food chain.

It's also currently far too expensive at about $20,000 (£12,000) a clone for the companies involved to even consider selling their prized animals as burgers.

'People are not producing clones for that purpose,' says Scott Davis, president of the US animal biotechnology company Viagen. Davis says that it is probably only the offspring of cloned animals that would be sold for meat.

Cloning could make sense for farmers as, in theory, it would allow them to easily produce lots of animals from a single prized specimen. A handful of American companies including Viagen are already producing cloned farm animals (mainly cows) for agriculture rather than scientific research. This prompted the US Food and Drug Administration to investigate the possible health risks, and in November 2003 it released its findings, saying that 'food products derived from animal clones and their offspring are likely to be as safe to eat as food from their non-clone counter-parts'.

It's currently far too expensive at about $20,000 (£12,000) a clone for the companies involved to even consider selling their prized animals as burgers

The defects and abnormalities that cloned animals can suffer have been well publicised since Dolly the sheep was created in 1996. Clones can suffer from abnormal growth, obesity and premature ageing, while Dolly herself was destroyed earlier this year after developing arthritis and a lung disease – unusual but not unheard of in a sheep that age.

Biotechnology companies developing cloned animals complain that these problems have been exaggerated as part of the campaign against human cloning, but Ian Wilmut, the geneticist who led the team that created Dolly, insists that they need to be considered before cloned meat is approved.

'I think it is extraordinarily unlikely that cloning would change an animal in such a way that food from it would be unhealthy to anyone who ate it. To me the greater issues are concerned with the welfare implications for the animals,' Wilmut says. 'The experience still is that there are considerable problems at birth and in some cases after birth for cloned animals. The exact details vary between species but I think as a generalisation that's still true.'

A spokesperson for the UK's Food Standards Agency says that meat from cloned animals would be classed as a novel food, so companies trying to sell it in Europe would require a special licence.

KEY FACTS

- The term clone, from the Greek for 'twig', denotes a group of identical entities; in recent years, 'clone' has come to mean a member of such a group and, in particular, an organism that is a genetic copy of an existing organism. (p. 2)

- As soon as a human individual exists, he or she has rights and interests relating to his or her own future – however long or short that future may be. Embryos have an interest in survival and protection from attack, just like any human being. (p. 5)

- Even if the clone were never to meet his or her original, the very awareness of such a person's existence would lead to a sense of living in the shadow of this unknown person. (p. 9)

- Education will change people's negative attitude towards human cloning. If we give human cloning a chance, it will most likely become a part of our daily lives. (p. 11)

- Although adult stem cells are found in many parts of the human body, embryonic stem cells have proven to be more flexible. Embryonic stem cells have the potential to develop into a wide range of tissue types and are called 'pluripotent'. (p. 13)

- Scientists have demonstrated for the first time that therapeutic cloning in humans can be achieved. The researchers in South Korea created 30 cloned embryos that grew to about 100 cells in size – further than any verified experiment so far. (p. 14)

- There has also been concern about the likelihood of 'designer' babies or the creation of a genetic sub-class. Wilder predictions include cloning dead people and people seeking eternal life by cloning themselves. (p. 15)

- The world's first Stem Cell Bank opened in the UK 19 May 2004. Under the controversial new project embryonic stem cells will be stored at the Bank and used for research into degenerative diseases such as Parkinson's, Alzheimer's and diabetes. (p. 16)

- Therapeutic cloning involves using cells from an individual to produce a cloned early embryo which is then used as a source of embryonic stem cells. (p. 17)

- Cloning human embryos to make babies is outlawed in Britain, but so-called therapeutic cloning, where embryos are created for research, was made legal under strict guidelines in 2002. (p. 22)

- The animal cloning era began in 1985 when Steen Willadsen, a Danish researcher, cloned a lamb from a sheep embryo. A cow cloned from embryo cells followed. The animals were cloned using a technique called nuclear transfer: the swapping of a cell nucleus into a hollowed-out unfertilised egg. (p. 25)

- There are two major concerns about the future of cloning technology. The first is whether it's ethically acceptable . . . the second is that the technology is far from perfect. (p. 26)

- When Dolly – the first cloned sheep – was born in 1997 she created world-wide headlines for the team of scientists at the Roslin Institute in Scotland whose test-tube techniques produced her. It seemed that flocks of cloned, genetically engineered sheep producing life-saving drugs in their milk might soon be grazing on farms. (p. 27)

- Dolly was a sensational sideline to this research. Her creation rewrote the laws of biology because she showed that ordinary (somatic) body cells could be turned back to embryos and made into new offspring, genetically identical to the animal whose cells had been used. (p. 29)

- Cloning is extremely inefficient and wasteful of animal lives. Hundreds of cloned embryos have to be created to produce just one or two live offspring. (p. 30)

- Reproductive cloning of animals is of no medical value for people. But it does illustrate some important biological principles. It shows that knowledge gained from one species does not usually translate to another. (p. 34)

- It is clear that cloning may cause a great deal of animal suffering. The so-called 'benefits', such as the production of genetically identical herds or flocks of animals for intensive farming, may be seen as dubious or even highly unethical. (p. 35)

- A mouse has been born that has two mothers, but no father. The animal, named Kaguya – which could prove as controversial as Dolly the cloned sheep – shows for the first time that a particular kind of 'virgin birth' is possible in mammals – and thus people. (p. 36)

- The key conclusion scientists reached in November 2003 was that cloned sheep, pigs and cows should be as safe to eat as their non-clone counterparts. And in our post BSE, intensively farmed world, take that whichever way you like. (p. 39)

ADDITIONAL RESOURCES

You might like to contact the following organisations for further information. Due to the increasing cost of postage, many organisations cannot respond to enquiries unless they receive a stamped, addressed envelope.

The Association of the British Pharmaceutical Industry (ABPI)
12 Whitehall
London, SW1A 2DY
Tel: 020 7930 3477
Fax: 020 7747 1414
Website: www.abpi.org.uk
The trade association for about a hundred companies in the UK producing prescription medicines.

The British Union for the Abolition of Vivisection (BUAV)
16a Crane Grove
London, N7 8NN
Tel: 020 7700 4888
Fax: 020 7700 0252
E-mail: info@buav.org
Website: www.buav.org
Believes animals are entitled to respect and compassion which animal experiments deny them.

Christian Medical Fellowship (CMF)
Partnership House
157 Waterloo Road
London, SE1 8XN
Tel: 020 7928 4694
Fax: 020 7620 2453
E-mail: admin@cmf.org.uk
Website: www.cmf.org.uk
Has over 4,500 British doctor members in all branches of medicine.

Dr Hadwen Trust for Humane Research
84a Tilehouse Street
Hitchin, SG5 2DY
Tel: 01462 436819
Fax: 01462 436844
E-mail: info@drhadwentrust.org.uk
Website: www.drhadwentrust.org.uk
Funds non-animal research into major health problems.

Europeans for Medical Advancement
P O Box 38604
London, W13 0YR
Tel: 020 8997 1265
Fax: 020 8997 1265
E-mail: efma@curedisease.com
Website: www.curedisease.com

Genetic Savings & Clone INC
80 Liberty Ship Way, Suite 22
Sausalito CA 94965
California, USA
Tel: + 1 415 289 2525
Fax: + 1 415 289 2526
E-mail: info@savingsandclone.com
Website: www.savingsandclone.com
Enriches the lives of pet lovers through superior cloning technologies.

Human Cloning Foundation
PMB 143
1100 Hammond Drive, Suite 410 A
Atlanta, GA 30328, USA
E-mail: HCloning@aol.com
Website: www.humancloning.org
Promotes education, awareness and research about human cloning and other forms of biotechnology.

Human Fertilisation & Embryology Authority (HFEA)
21 Bloomsbury Street
London, WC1B 3HF
Tel: 020 7291 8200
Fax: 020 7291 8201
E-mail: admin@hfea.gov.uk
Website: www.hfea.gov.uk
HFEA is a non-departmental Government body that regulates and inspects all UK clinics providing IVF, donor insemination or the storage of eggs, sperm or embryos.

The Linacre Centre for Healthcare Ethics
60 Grove End Road
St Johns Wood
London, NW8 9NH
Tel: 020 7806 4088
Fax: 020 7266 5424
E-mail: admin@linacre.org
Website: www.linacre.org
The Linacre Centre exists to help Catholics, and others, explore and understand the Church's position on bioethical issues.

ProLife Party
PO Box 13395
London, SW3 6XE
Tel: 020 7581 6939
Fax: 020 7581 3868
E-mail: info@prolife.org.uk
Website: www.prolife.org.uk
The ProLife Party is Europe's first Pro-Life Political Party.

Research Defence Society (RDS)
25 Shaftsbury Avenue
London, W1D 7EG
Tel: 020 7287 2818
Fax: 020 7287 2627
E-mail: admin@rds-online.org.uk
Website: www.rds-online.org.uk
Represents medical researchers in the public debate about the use of animals in medical research and testing.

Society, Religion and Technology Project
Church of Scotland,
John Knox House, 45 High Street
Edinburgh, EH1 1SR
Tel: 0131 556 2953
Fax: 0131 556 7478
E-mail: srtp@srtp.org.uk
Website: www.srtp.org.uk
Has been in the forefront of the debate on animal and human cloning since 1996.

The Wellcome Trust
The Wellcome Building
183 Euston Road
London, NW1 2BE
Tel: 020 7611 8888
Fax: 020 7611 8545
E-mail: contact@wellcome.ac.uk
Website: www.wellcome.ac.uk
The Wellcome Trust's mission is 'to foster and promote research with the aim of improving human and animal health'.

World Health Organization (WHO)
20 Avenue Appia
1211-Geneva 27
Switzerland
Tel: + 41 22 791 2111
Fax: + 41 22 791 3111
E-mail: info@who.ch
Website: www.who.int
WHO works to make a difference in the lives of the world's people by enhancing both life expectancy and health expectancy.

INDEX

ACKNOWLEDGEMENTS

The publisher is grateful for permission to reproduce the following material.

While every care has been taken to trace and acknowledge copyright, the publisher tenders its apology for any accidental infringement or where copyright has proved untraceable. The publisher would be pleased to come to a suitable arrangement in any such case with the rightful owner.

Chapter One: Human Cloning

Human reproductive cloning, © The Association of the British Pharmaceutical Industry (ABPI), *Questions on cloning*, © World Health Organization (WHO), *Adult cell or reproductive cloning*, © The Association of the British Pharmaceutical Industry (ABPI), *Human cloning* © ProLife Party, *Cloning*, © The Linacre Centre for Healthcare Ethics, *Why is it dangerous to clone humans?*, © Guardian Newspapers Limited 2004, *Scientists lobby the UN to ban cloning*, © Telegraph Group Limited, London 2004, *Cloning is beneficial*, © Human Cloning Foundation, *Stem cell research*, © Human Fertilisation & Embryology Authority (HFEA), *European attitudes to six applications of biotechnology in 2002*, © European Opinion Research Group, *Cloned human embryos are stem cell breakthrough*, © Reed Business Information Ltd., *Why is using stem cells controversial?*, © Crown copyright is reproduced with the permission of Her Majesty's Stationery Office, *First stem cell bank opens in UK*, © Associated Newspapers Ltd 2004, *Therapeutic or biomedical cloning*, © The Association of the British Pharmaceutical Industry (ABPI), *Korean clones – unsafe, unnecessary and unethical*, © 2004 Christian Medical Fellowship, *Cloned embryo research poses ethical problems*, © Society, Religion and Technology Project, *Cloning and stem cells*, © Reed Business Information Ltd., *Milestones in UK stem cell related research and regulation*, © The Wellcome Trust, *Human embryo research plan is first of its kind*, © Guardian Newspapers Limited 2004, *Embryo cloning*, © The Association of the British Pharmaceutical Industry (ABPI), *A case for cloning*, © The Observer, *Scientists get go-ahead to clone first human embryo*, © Telegraph Group Limited, London 2004

Chapter Two: Animal Cloning

The world of science fiction, © Telegraph Group Limited, London 2004, *Cloning concerns*, © 2004 cherrybyte.org, *Embryos for medical research*, © MORI, *Should we clone animals?*, © Society, Religion and Technology Project, *Animal cloning*, © Dr Hadwen Trust for Humane Research, *Animal cloning*, © Research Defence Society (RDS), *Endangered species gain a place on Frozen Ark*, © Telegraph Group Limited, London 2004, *Cloning*, © Europeans for Medical Advancement, *Genetics*, © BUAV, *Mouse with two mothers and no father*, © Telegraph Group Limited, London 2004, *You only live twice*, © 2004 Scotsman.com, *Pet cloning*, © 2004 Genetic Savings & Clone, *Cloned food*, © Guardian Newspapers Limited 2004.

Photographs and illustrations:

Pages 1, 18, 25, 29, 38: Simon Kneebone; pages 5, 26, 34: Don Hatcher; pages 6, 14, 31: Bev Aisbett; pages 8, 20, 28, 33: Angelo Madrid; pages 10, 36: Pumpkin House.

Craig Donnellan
Cambridge
September, 2004